THE PRACTITIONER

Marilyn Cochran-Smith and S

Repositioning Educational Leadership: Practitioners Leading from an Inquiry Stance
JAMES H. LYTLE, SUSAN L. LYTLE, MICHAEL C. JOHANEK, & KATHY J. RHO, EDS.

Professional Development in Relational Learning Communities: Teachers in Connection
MIRIAM B. RAIDER-ROTH

Impactful Practitioner Inquiry: The Ripple Effect on Classrooms, Schools, and Teacher Professionalism
SUE NICHOLS & PHIL CORMACK

Teaching in Themes: An Approach to Schoolwide Learning, Creating Community, and Differentiating Instruction
DEBORAH MEIER, MATTHEW KNOESTER, & KATHERINE CLUNIS D'ANDREA, EDS.

Family Dialogue Journals: School–Home Partnerships That Support Student Learning
JOBETH ALLEN, JENNIFER BEATY, ANGELA DEAN, JOSEPH JONES, STEPHANIE SMITH MATHEWS, JEN MCCREIGHT, ELYSE SCHWEDLER, & AMBER M. SIMMONS

Raising Race Questions: Whiteness and Inquiry in Education
ALI MICHAEL

Making Space for Active Learning: The Art and Practice of Teaching
ANNE C. MARTIN & ELLEN SCHWARTZ, EDS.

The First Year of Teaching: Classroom Research to Increase Student Learning
JABARI MAHIRI & SARAH WARSHAUER FREEDMAN, EDS.

A Critical Inquiry Framework for K–12 Teachers: Lessons and Resources from the U.N. Rights of the Child
JOBETH ALLEN & LOIS ALEXANDER, EDS.

Democratic Education in Practice: Inside the Mission Hill School
MATTHEW KNOESTER

Action Research in Special Education: An Inquiry Approach for Effective Teaching and Learning
SUSAN M. BRUCE & GERALD J. PINE

Inviting Families into the Classroom: Learning from a Life in Teaching
LYNNE YERMANOCK STRIEB

Jt... ...y. Taking the Long View of the Child —Prospect's Philosophy in Action
PATRICIA F. CARINI & MARGARET HIMLEY, WITH CAROL CHRISTINE, CECILIA ESPINOSA, & JULIA FOURNIER

Acting Out! Combating Homophobia Through Teacher Activism
MOLLIE V. BLACKBURN, CAROLINE T. CLARK, LAUREN M. KENNEY, & JILL M. SMITH, EDS.

Puzzling Moments, Teachable Moments: Practicing Teacher Research in Urban Classrooms
CYNTHIA BALLENGER

Inquiry as Stance: Practitioner Research for the Next Generation
MARILYN COCHRAN-SMITH & SUSAN L. LYTLE

Building Racial and Cultural Competence in the Classroom: Strategies from Urban Educators
KAREN MANHEIM TEEL & JENNIFER OBIDAH, EDS.

Re-Reading Families: The Literate Lives of Urban Children, Four Years Later
CATHERINE COMPTON-LILLY

"What About Rose?" Using Teacher Research to Reverse School Failure
SMOKEY WILSON

Immigrant Students and Literacy: Reading, Writing, and Remembering
GERALD CAMPANO

Going Public with Our Teaching: An Anthology of Practice
THOMAS HATCH, DILRUBA AHMED, ANN LIEBERMAN, DEBORAH FAIGENBAUM, MELISSA EILER WHITE, & DÉSIRÉE H. POINTER MACE, EDS.

Teaching as Inquiry: Asking Hard Questions to Improve Practice and Student Achievement
ALEXANDRA WEINBAUM, DAVID ALLEN, TINA BLYTHE, KATHERINE SIMON, STEVE SEIDEL, & CATHERINE RUBIN

"Is This English?" Race, Language, and Culture in the Classroom
BOB FECHO

Teacher Research for Better Schools
MARIAN M. MOHR, COURTNEY ROGERS, BETSY SANFORD, MARY ANN NOCERINO, MARION S. MACLEAN, & SHEILA CLAWSON

(continued)

Imagination and Literacy:
A Teacher's Search for the Heart of Learning
Karen Gallas

Regarding Children's Words:
Teacher Research on Language and Literacy
Brookline Teacher Researcher Seminar

Rural Voices: Place-Conscious Education and the Teaching of Writing
Robert E. Brooke, Ed.

Teaching Through the Storm: A Journal of Hope
Karen Hale Hankins

Reading Families:
The Literate Lives of Urban Children
Catherine Compton-Lilly

Narrative Inquiry in Practice:
Advancing the Knowledge of Teaching
Nona Lyons & Vicki Kubler LaBoskey, Eds.

Starting Strong: A Different Look at Children, Schools, and Standards
Patricia F. Carini

Because of the Kids: Facing Racial and Cultural Differences in Schools
Jennifer E. Obidah & Karen Manheim Teel

Ethical Issues in Practitioner Research
Jane Zeni, Ed.

Action, Talk, and Text:
Learning and Teaching Through Inquiry
Gordon Wells, Ed.

Teaching Mathematics to the New Standards:
Relearning the Dance
Ruth M. Heaton

Teacher Narrative as Critical Inquiry:
Rewriting the Script
Joy S. Ritchie & David E. Wilson

From Another Angle:
Children's Strengths and School Standards
Margaret Himley with Patricia F. Carini, Eds.

Inside City Schools: Investigating
Literacy in the Multicultural Classroom
Sarah Warshauer Freedman, Elizabeth Radin Simons, Julie Shalhope Kalnin, Alex Casareno, & the M-Class Teams

Class Actions: Teaching for Social Justice in Elementary and Middle School
JoBeth Allen, Ed.

Teacher/Mentor:
A Dialogue for Collaborative Learning
Peg Graham, Sally Hudson-Ross, Chandra Adkins, Patti McWhorter, & Jennifer McDuffie Stewart, Eds.

Teaching Other People's Children: Literacy and Learning in a Bilingual Classroom
Cynthia Ballenger

Teaching, Multimedia, and Mathematics:
Investigations of Real Practice
Magdalene Lampert & Deborah Loewenberg Ball

John Dewey and the Challenge of Classroom Practice
Stephen M. Fishman & Lucille McCarthy

"Sometimes I Can Be Anything":
Power, Gender, and Identity in a Primary Classroom
Karen Gallas

Learning in Small Moments:
Life in an Urban Classroom
Daniel R. Meier

Repositioning Educational Leadership

Practitioners Leading from an Inquiry Stance

James H. Lytle
Susan L. Lytle
Michael C. Johanek
Kathy J. Rho
Editors

Published by Teachers College Press, 1234 Amsterdam Avenue, New York, NY 10027

Library of Congress Cataloging-in-Publication Data

Names: Lytle, James H., 1940– editor. | Lytle, Susan H., editor. | Johanek, Michael C., editor. | Rho, Kathy J., editor.
Title: Repositioning educational leadership : practitioners leading from an inquiry stance / edited by James H. Lytle, Susan H. Lytle, Michael C. Johanek, and Kathy J. Rho.
Description: New York, NY : Teachers College Press, [2018] | Series: The practitioner inquiry series | Includes index. |
Identifiers: LCCN 2018021457 (print) | LCCN 2018031017 (ebook) | ISBN 9780807777046 (ebook) | ISBN 9780807759448 (hardcover : alk. paper) | ISBN 9780807759226 (pbk. : alk. paper) | ISBN 9780807777046 (ebk.)
Subjects: LCSH: Educational leadership—United States. | Educational change—United States.
Classification: LCC LB2805 (ebook) | LCC LB2805 .R453 2018 (print) | DDC 371.2—dc23
LC record available at https://lccn.loc.gov/2018021457

ISBN 978-0-8077-5922-6 (paper)
ISBN 978-0-8077-5944-8 (hardcover)
ISBN 978-0-8077-7704-6 (ebook)

Printed on acid-free paper
Manufactured in the United States of America

25 24 23 22 21 20 19 18 8 7 6 5 4 3 2 1

Contents

Acknowledgments

We the editors have had the great pleasure of working with our practitioner scholar colleagues, both students and alumni, from the University of Pennsylvania's Mid-Career Doctoral Program community for more years than we wish to admit, now numbering over 400 leaders across the country and, increasingly, across the globe. We continue to learn from their insightful, committed, and complex work, and we wish to express our deep gratitude for their generous engagement as a community. This publication reflects our effort to bring greater visibility to their work, and to invite the wider field into dialogue. The response from this community to the initial proposal for this volume was stunning, an outpouring of interest from those we know already have excessively demanding day jobs. We were truly inspired by their commitment to do the work, not just at their respective sites, but at the level of the field, taking the time and energy to engage colleagues also wrestling with the privilege and challenge of educational leadership today.

This book project could not have happened, of course, without the dedicated participation of the 11 practitioner scholars who authored its respective chapters. This has not been a quick process, as we also leveraged this project as an inquiry into what it means to reposition educational leadership by exploring the practice of leading from an inquiry stance. The authors' willingness to persist in this dialogue, over several years now, testifies to their generosity, their commitment, and their abiding sense of humor.

Among the editors, we also wish to acknowledge the critical role played by our colleague, Dr. Kathy Rho. She combines—rarely, in our experience—both a keen editorial eye and a universe-ordering sense of organization. We would simply not have advanced to completion without her insightful and wise shepherding of our collective work.

We have also been fortunate to have the guidance and collaboration of our talented editorial colleagues at Teachers College Press. In particular, we thank Brian Ellerbeck for his early encouragement of this volume and Sarah Biondello for thoughtfully steering us to greater clarity and completion.

We each also acknowledge that a project of this sort and duration benefits mightily from the patience and support of family and friends. We know well your innumerable contributions and remain in your debt.

We see this volume as a beginning. As the chapters make evident, the richness of the work warrants our sustained—and collective—inquiry. We invite you into what we hope is an enduring inquiry into the messiness of the leadership endeavor in educating institutions, anchored in and inspired by the invaluable perspectives of those actually doing the work. We welcome your ongoing engagement via the website accompanying and supporting this volume. Join us at repositioningedleadership.org to learn more.

We look forward to engaging you in this work, and thank all those who have made this possible.

Repositioning Educational Leadership

Practitioners Leading from an Inquiry Stance

Introduction

An Educating Leadership

Context shapes leadership in dramatic ways. Yet the approaches urged upon leaders through top-down policies often ignore obvious complexities of educational institutions and the people they serve. Seldom are the voices heard of those trying to make sense of these complexities. Each day, educational leaders learn anew of their community, its particular emotional contours and messy humanity. At their very best, perhaps their aspirational best, many proceed each day collaboratively and thoughtfully, consensually yet decisively, wrestling with the often-hidden, sloppy, real worlds of their day-to-day practice.

Leaders need opportunities to learn from the "inside" of other leaders' experiences, doubts and all. This volume addresses that need. Here is the work of 11 colleagues, reflecting the perceptions and experiences of those doing the work, toward shared inquiry as leaders and those supporting leaders. This is the real work, in its uncertainty and messiness.

This book is an invitation into their contexts, and into this wider community of practice. It takes as its premise that educational leadership for K–12 schools is increasingly complicated, as demands on educational leaders and schools continue to escalate. Much of the policy and published work on educational leadership in the past decade has focused on instructional leadership and performance standards for prospective and current administrators. The expectation seems to be that the work of school leaders is to manage schools, attend to the standards, and implement the policies that their states, school boards, or superintendents direct. From our point of view, such expectations undervalue school leaders and limit their roles. Relatively little attention has been given to leaders' work from their vantage points—how school and district leaders conceptualize their roles, how and what they are learning, and how they are posing and solving problems of practice. This volume brings their voices to the table.

RATIONALE FOR THE BOOK

The contributors to *Repositioning Educational Leadership* argue collectively that when school, district, and other educational leaders position themselves as inquirers, their leadership can illuminate and improve many aspects of institutional life and create intellectually demanding and rich learning environments—for both adults and children. Key to this assertion is the potential for site-based leaders to identify (often with their colleagues, students, and parents in the community) issues and problems that are *locally* significant, previously unrecognized, and rarely given the systematic, intentional study that an inquiry-based approach to leadership affords. Building from the premise that a good portion of what we need to know about the complex practices of leadership remains largely hidden and untapped, this volume surfaces evidence that this approach to knowledge generation in educational leadership is not only productive for the specific educational institutions involved, but also useful for the field more broadly.

Dialogic and ongoing, *leading from an inquiry stance* differs from the diagnostic, evaluative, and summative approaches to data collection and decisionmaking common in today's climate of top-down accountability. From the perspective of prominent conceptual frameworks of leadership, *inquiry as stance* approaches what Heifetz and Linsky (2002) call "adaptive leadership," differentiating between "technical problems" and "adaptive challenges" (p. 14). Technical problems can be solved with a high degree of certainty by applying current know-how. People expect those in charge to know what to do, and those in charge think that leading means accepting responsibility for solving the problems.

But the complex problems that educational leaders/practitioners often confront need to be considered "adaptive challenges," those that "require experiments, new discoveries, and adjustments from numerous places in the organization or community" (2002, p. 13). Heifetz and Linsky explain that "without learning new ways—changing attitudes, values, and behaviors—people cannot make the adaptive leap necessary to thrive in [a] new environment" (p. 13).

The practitioner-authors in this volume both embody and grapple with these concepts. In determining the focus of their chapters, they have avoided tempting but insufficient technical solutions; taken time to read and understand the contexts relating to the matters they are considering; established trust with colleagues and stakeholders; and worked toward "learning new ways" of thinking, being, and doing. In other words, they have tried to lead from an inquiry stance. As the 11 chapters illustrate, doing this requires that leaders acknowledge their uncertainty, foster collaboration, and take an inquiring stance in relationship to the challenges and problems they have determined to take on. As editors, we offer them not as exemplars, recipes, or models but as invitations to the productive possibilities of this approach.

In many of the chapters, questions are posed about issues rarely recognized for their importance to the success of a school or district. These inquiries respect the purposes and processes of problem-posing (Freire, 1970) within a local context, and create structures that entail listening to and valuing the perspectives and experiences of all involved. The chapter authors write frankly about their own positionality, their own "dis-ease" (Greene, 1995/2000), as well as display an openness and intent to question assumptions formed from experiences they have had as leaders.

In developing the book, we have learned that the essence of what it means to lead from an inquiry stance emerges from the questions or problems posed, as we see in each chapter. The framing of the problem is enhanced by what gets asked, to/by whom, why, and by the ways that the leader and his/her colleagues/students/community try to understand and add their own perspectives to the issue. Who gets consulted or included in the inquiry varies among the chapters. For example, are students, teachers, staff, and/or community involved in the processes of problem-posing? Who does the sense-making from the information gathered, and how is that accomplished? What does it mean to learn from these inquiries; that is, what counts as findings or learnings?

Addressing the equity and ethical dimensions of their inquiry stance, the author-leaders write about their willingness to ask questions that might make them uncomfortable or vulnerable. Problem-posing, according to this approach to leadership, is not just about curiosity or attention to top-down policies. An inquiry stance includes a willingness to question normative assumptions and practices. These leaders do what Anderson and Jones (2000) call making an effort to "problematize taken-for-granted aspects of organizational life" (p. 449). Sometimes, leading from an inquiry stance disrupts one's own identity and/or the shared identity of an institution or organization. Professional courage must be summoned. The process of inquiry does not just reveal what is invisible but also acknowledges and invites questions that might be disruptive to who one is and what the institution/organization represents. This "constructive disruption" (Cochran-Smith & Lytle, 2009) is contingent on the positionality of the leader and the degree to which leaders are aware of their position in relation to the problem posed.

The authors bring to their inquiry-based leadership narratives a set of lenses that were developed over time as they grappled with their various roles as educational leaders. Their differing contexts and histories inform those lenses. Additionally, these contributors pose and work on problems within schools and districts based in part on how they understand the larger context—the world outside their "walls," including various aspects of school or system culture, community expectations, or top-down policies. In addition, the authors ask questions about their contexts that others, external to that environment, may (or may not) think are significant. As a consequence of taking an inquiry stance as a leader, these authors may alert readers to important dimensions of leadership practice that were previously not a part of the reader's experience, studies, or frameworks.

Readers will ask themselves: What does this "inside" account allow me to see in my own context? Would this stance of inquiry lead to improvement in the organizations in which I work? How do I define improvement? Am I open to interrogating how I understand this concept/practice/issue and to learning from my peers how others understand and interpret it? The chapters invite readers to pay attention to *learning as a leader,* and thus to take a stance of "vulnerability and curiosity" (McCarthy, 2014).

Each of the authors implicitly embraces uncertainty as both a necessary and a generative condition of the world of leading. It makes possible an openness to learning and to withholding judgment so that the unimagined and the unfamiliar can enter the learning space. The leader-contributors do not intend a state of vagueness or perpetual indeterminacy. They seek, rather, to leverage uncertainty in the service of transformative leadership, inviting themselves and others to learn about the familiar in unfamiliar ways. These leaders' narratives make space for new questions and perspectives to emerge. In practice, their inquiry stance intentionally creates spaces for organizational learning, creating the conditions for productive dissonance, a kind of *leaderly* openness.

INQUIRY AS STANCE

Our work has a genealogy.

We frame the notion of practitioners leading from an inquiry stance conceptually in Cochran-Smith and Lytle's (2009) theory of inquiry as stance. According to this framework:

> Inquiry as stance is perspectival and conceptual—a worldview, a critical habit of mind, a dynamic way of knowing and being in the world of educational practice that carries across professional careers and educational settings. (p. 120)

This stance acknowledges and relies upon the "collective intellectual capacity of practitioners," viewing it as fundamental to the enrichment of practice and community (p. 121). The framework invites educators to regard their schools, districts, and communities as sites of knowledge generation, occurring within particular social, historical, cultural, and political contexts. An inquiry stance

> foregrounds the role that practitioners can play, both individually and collectively, in generating local knowledge, re-envisioning and theorizing practice, as well as interpreting and interrogating the theory and research of others. (p. 127)

Such an enhanced role for practitioners carries implications, as it can

> make problematic current arrangements of practice, the ways knowledge is constructed, evaluated, and used in various educational settings, and the roles [leaders] play in facilitating change in their own work contexts. (p. 127)

In this book, we use the concept of inquiry as stance to signal an active and critical interrogation of systems, structures, and practices—a focus on problem-posing and seeking new understandings in systematic and intentional ways. Such a stance requires the ongoing suspension of knowing, up front, what will happen, and thus an approach to leadership that relies on the strategic use of uncertainty to create the conditions for ongoing inquiry. This opens a space for rethinking fundamental assumptions about the intellectual (social and political) activity of leading and for reconstructing leadership practice as inquiry across the professional lifespan. Cochran-Smith and Lytle (2009) note:

> Fundamental to the notion of inquiry as stance is the idea that educational practice is not simply instrumental in the sense of figuring out how to get things done, but also and more importantly, it is social and political in the sense of deliberating about what gets done, why to get it done, who decides, and whose interests are served. (p. 121)

At the level of assumptions, inquiry insists that

> a core part of the knowledge and expertise necessary for transforming practice and enhancing students' learning resides in the questions, theories, and strategies generated collectively by practitioners themselves and in their joint interrogations of the knowledge, practice and theories of others. (pp. 121–124)

Leaders may need to form communities of inquiry within their work settings that engage in the following practices:

> Collaboratively reconsidering what is taken for granted; challenging school, classroom and other institutional structures; deliberating about what it means to know and what is regarded as expert knowledge; rethinking educational categories; constructing and reconstructing interpretive frameworks for making sense of information; revising and creating curricula and syllabi; and attempting to uncover the values and interests served, and not served, by the current arrangements of schooling. (p. 142)

Leading from an inquiry stance, then, seeks change that serves democratic purposes and social justice ends, which are fundamental to our societal values in education. This means equity of learning opportunities for all students, commitment to participatory processes, and working both within and against the system as an ongoing effort to problematize fundamental assumptions about the purposes and consequences of the existing educational system.

GENESIS OF THE BOOK

As with any work, this initiative arises out of a particular human community, a collective effort growing out of the editors' and contributors' shared experience in an executive format doctoral program for veteran educational leaders from across the country. Members of the University of Pennsylvania's intensive Mid-Career Doctoral Program in Educational Leadership include experienced principals, independent school heads, department heads, teacher-leaders, charter school founders, superintendents, national association leaders, entrepreneurs, state education department administrators, and other leaders in the pre-K–12 world. Each school leader brings on average 18 years of experience to the table. The community of students, alumni, program faculty, and associates represents an intentionally-sought, presumption-challenging diversity of race, gender, age, discipline, position, locale, ideology, geography, and career path. The cohort format grounds the work in mutual respect across the differences of background, perspective, and context, while modeling the engagement of peers in problem-posing and dialogic inquiry. Individuals bring their experiences and knowledge to this trusted space, where the realities of uncertainty can get voiced and engaged. Remaining full-time within the complexity of their daily practice, students in this cohort-based program learn about and engage in professional, site-based inquiries throughout the 3 years of their coursework. For one weekend each month, identifying and investigating significant problems that emerge from their everyday practice, they contribute to educational improvement within both their own settings and those of their colleagues.

The doctoral program thus provides unusual opportunities for participation in professional learning communities that focus on various iterations of practitioner inquiry. Participation in these communities offers a space for posing questions and deepening participants' understandings of critical issues in leadership broadly and in their own leadership specifically. This affords students, faculty, and alumni, who are seasoned professionals, an ongoing site for critically examining their own assumptions, issues, and questions of practice. This volume tries to capture and share some of this ongoing work, providing—the contributors hope—a window into the rich reflections that arise within this trusted "third space" of practitioner-scholars. (For more information about the Mid-Career Doctoral Program in Educational Leadership and its initiatives, see Appendix B.)

LENSES FOR READING THE BOOK

As we have already mentioned, the development of *Repositioning Educational Leadership* was driven by the editors' awareness that the mid-career administrators we were teaching were writing papers and doing dissertations that demonstrated intriguing insights into the connections between leadership and inquiry. When we put out a call for chapters for a possible book documenting their work, we were amazed by the enthusiastic response: Almost 40 former students submitted preliminary proposals.

In our call we had not stipulated what prospective contributions would need to include, other than that they explore how inquiry informed their day-to-day leadership. Nor did we stipulate a theory or research base that should underpin their contributions. As we read through the submissions and worked toward a final set of practitioner-authored chapters, we were also engaged in an inquiry of our own—what would inquiry look like and mean to contributors, and how might they draw on the leadership literature in creating and interpreting their narratives?

We gradually became aware that although much of educational leadership literature of the last 2 decades has focused on establishing links between specific leadership activities and student achievement, that was not what our practitioner-authors chose to write about. Instead, their submissions picked up other threads or themes from the leadership literature: relational trust, complexity, uncertainty, understanding one's context/environment, leading learning, and leading for equity/social justice. We provide brief summaries of pertinent literature and examples from the practitioners' inquiries to connect these threads to the leadership and organizational literature.

Relational Trust

The importance of relational trust is a core theme of *Organizing Schools for Improvement: Lessons from Chicago* (Bryk, Sebring, Allensworth, Luppescu, & Easton, 2010). In the explanatory model that emerges from the authors' research, leadership is the driver for student outcomes (engagement and academic learning) and is mediated by the extent of relational trust the leader establishes across the school community, which in turn relates to the leader's ability to understand and operate in the local school community context. Bryk and his colleagues find "powerful relationships" among school leadership, relational trust, and school improvement. To create relational trust,

> Principals establish both respect and personal regard . . . when they acknowledge the vulnerability of others, actively listen to their concerns, and eschew arbitrary actions . . . Absent such trust, it is nearly impossible for schools to develop and sustain the strength . . . for sustaining the hard work of school improvement. (p. 207)

In several of the chapters that follow, the leaders speak of building trusting relationships with Asian, Latino, White, and African American students that create space for the students to share anxieties and concerns about their school experiences. The students' comments then become the "data" informing the leader's work with faculty and support staff, within and beyond the immediate setting. In another chapter, an elementary principal explains how she developed sufficient trust with faculty who then were able to share their approaches to engaging students without fear of embarrassment or reprisal.

Understanding Context

Wahlstrom and her colleagues (2010), in what they describe as "the largest study of [educational leader efficacy] conducted to date in the United States," argue that understanding context is essential (p. 11). Understanding context means how leaders learn about the circumstances in which they find themselves, the underlying causes of the problems they encounter, and how they respond adaptively to those problems.

The chapter authored by a career changer provides a persuasive example. He chronicles his transition from corporate finance to school district senior management, and explains how he went about learning the community, district organization, central office personnel and culture, the schools, parents, and students, as well as state policy and decisionmakers. A female administrator at a Catholic all-boys school exemplifies a different sort of contextual awareness in her chapter. In response to her sense that many female teachers in their network were feeling isolated and unheard, she initiated a series of discussions about how gender affected the ways they were perceived and treated by students and colleagues.

Uncertainty and Complexity

Another dimension evident in the practitioners' chapters is the complexity and uncertainty of educational leadership—as policy, politics, community, markets, and technology evolve and interact in the pre-K–12 education sector (see J. Lytle & Sokoloff, 2013). The challenges educational and other organizational leaders deal with are examined in the "embracing complexity" issue of *Harvard Business Review* (see Sargut & McGrath, 2011); the authors stipulate that

> complex organizations are far more difficult to manage than merely complicated ones. It's harder to predict what will happen, because complex systems interact in unexpected ways. It's harder to make sense of things, because the degree of complexity may lie beyond our cognitive limits. (p. 68)

As an illustration, one chapter author, head of an all-boys urban charter school, describes learning that an assembly intended to raise student awareness about respectful treatment of girls and women instead became a chaotic shouting match. How, he wondered, should he respond? How had he misread school and community culture? How could he repair the fragmentation and anger roiling the school? In another chapter, the author, an assistant superintendent in a state department of education, acknowledges her uncertainty as she tries to make her division more responsive to the diverse array of local education agencies it serves—and simultaneously deals with repeated turnover in the state superintendent's office.

Leading Learning

It isn't only developing trust, dealing with uncertainty, or learning the context that matters. As Morgan (1997) explains, "organizational members must be skilled in understanding the paradigms, metaphors, mind-sets, or mental models that underpin how the organization operates" (p. 92). For this sort of learning to occur, "organizations must develop cultures that support change and risk-taking . . . promote an openness that encourages dialogue and the expression of conflicting points of view" (p. 94). That argument suggests why educational leaders must be "leaders of learning."

An elementary school principal illustrates this learning leadership in her chapter, explaining how and why she created small learning communities for faculty—to describe and consider the interests and strengths of individual students and collaboratively determine how to build on those interests and strengths. A rural district superintendent provides a different example of "leading learning," describing how he helped the community articulate its hopes for its children and then led them through a series of meetings, seminars, and readings to expand their sense of possibilities.

Leading for Equity and Social Justice

Democratic purposes and social justice ends are illustrated in the case of an urban high school principal whose school highlights its college-prep mission. She later hears from graduates who felt unprepared for what they encountered in college, raising doubts about her own leadership and design elements of the school. Another chapter author learned that many of her school's minority students perceived a deeply-rooted component of the academic assessment process as demeaning and discriminatory. Her challenge was to create faculty awareness of the problem and then collaboratively determine how feedback to students could be managed in more sensitive and constructive ways.

In the next section, we briefly describe a range of approaches to the subject of practitioner inquiry/research in the educational leadership literature. Our purpose is to suggest some of the ways this topic has been variously interpreted and used in university-based research, program design, and professional development for leaders and ultimately to distinguish leading from an inquiry stance as a distinct approach, one that we believe can add usefully to the ongoing conversation.

PRACTITIONER INQUIRY IN THE LEADERSHIP LITERATURE

Surveying the landscape of investigations into practice by practitioners reveals a diverse array of research traditions and social movements from which different forms of practice-based inquiry have developed (Zeichner, 2001). In the field of education broadly construed, some use the term *practitioner inquiry* as the conceptual umbrella (e.g., Cochran-Smith & Lytle, 2004) while others prefer *action research* or *practitioner research* (e.g., Anderson, Herr, & Nihlen, 1994; 2007; Zeichner, 2001). Depending on their particular theoretical framing and context, some elect more specific terminology such as critical action research, teacher research, self-study, participative inquiry, narrative inquiry, reflective practice, participatory action research, or autobiographical inquiry, among others.

Each of these descriptors also implicitly references a range of historical, epistemological, and political sources. In short, there is no commonly accepted language or agreed-upon definition for inquiry by practitioners in their site of practice, but rather a rich array of evolving perceptions and inventions of what this kind of work looks like, means, and might mean going forward.

Much of what we have in the practitioner inquiry/leadership literature is in the tradition(s) of action research, although definitions and interpretations vary. There are at least two comprehensive edited handbooks of educational action research: *The Handbook of Action Research: Participative Inquiry and Practice* edited by Reason and Bradbury (2001) and *The SAGE Handbook of Educational Action Research* edited by Noffke and Somekh (2009). Most of the chapters in these two books pertain to the evolution and variation in perspectives of the field; of the 86 chapters in these two handbooks, however, only one focuses specifically on the relationship of practitioner inquiry and leadership.

In this section, we thus look at published accounts that explicitly link the concept of practitioner inquiry/research with the work of leaders and leadership, and then use this brief review of the literature to further clarify what we mean by *leading from an inquiry stance* as the organizing framework for this book. This review breaks out into seven areas:

- Design of doctoral programs and dissertations
- Reconceptualizing research and scholarship in doctoral programs
- Leaders as applied researchers
- Resources for action research dissertation writers
- Principal professional development as action research
- Generating knowledge from sites of practice
- Leader-authored accounts of inquiry/research

Design of Doctoral Programs and Dissertations

Most of the academic literature on leadership, and on leaders as inquirers or researchers of their own contexts, focuses on faculty expectations for dissertation research in specific doctoral programs in educational administration. Based on an exploratory survey of faculty in educational administration programs, Osterman, Furman, and Sernak (2014), however, found that action research dissertations are actually used infrequently to meet dissertation requirements because of faculties' expressed "lack of conceptual clarity" about the nature of action research and concerns about its "methodological legitimacy" (p. 88).

In their own program, nevertheless, the authors support what they call "a participatory model of action research" with emphasis on involving doctoral students in change efforts, developing collaborative leadership skills, and taking a social justice perspective (p. 89). In their view, action research should not be evaluated primarily by rigor or methodology but rather by criteria such as inclusivity and engagement in organizational learning communities. They argue that well-designed action research would then meet basic standards for scientific rigor.

Reconceptualizing Research and Scholarship in Doctoral Programs

Also from the perspective of faculty in educational administration doctoral programs, Riehl, Larson, Short, and Reitzug (2000) take on the challenge of trying to "reconceptualize" research and scholarship in leadership education. They propose that the two communities of practice in the field—academics and practitioners—should endeavor to become a single community of scholars. To do this, they argue for more attention to practitioners' interests and to the knowledge they bring to programs, what they call an "epistemology of practice." The issue here is not so much what counts as knowledge but rather what knowledge is needed in the field. Quoting Donmoyer (1999), they stipulate that

> opening up inquiry in educational administration to access and document the knowledge of practitioners can counter the notion that the current knowledge base is only a figment of academic researchers' imagination, which has been designed to justify their own privileged positions as "experts" in the field. (p. 395)

Rather than aim for generalizations, Riehl et al. argue that "practical research" can "provide new ways of thinking about practice and help generate new questions" (p. 398). Connecting to the work of Anderson and Herr (1999), they explore what they consider important aspects of "practical research"—including the insider status of the researcher and the centrality of action to the questions being asked. The authors ultimately advocate for blurring the boundaries between what they call conventional and practical research toward the creation of "new genres" accountable to both audiences—drawn together by "the practice of scholarship." Thus, doctoral students would be encouraged "to think about scholars and scholarly practice in new ways" (p. 413).

Leaders as Applied Researchers

In another provocative take on leadership scholarship by practicing leaders in doctoral programs, Lochmiller and Lester (2017) posit what they call a "working model of practitioner-scholarship," arguing that what is most needed is a conceptual framework for this new genre, one that positions the doctoral student/practitioner to focus on understanding local problems of practice through a process of in-depth inquiry. This requires that all program faculty "take a learning orientation" and that students' research opportunities emerge from their practice of leadership in schools and districts.

From this perspective, leadership programs should emphasize "consistency, rigor and theoretical depth" in training educational leadership students in methods of research. Departing from a strict emphasis on the "action" in action research, Lochmiller and Lester emphasize that the understanding of educational problems "involves intervening in educational settings and programs for the benefit of students, teachers and other stakeholders" (p. 12). Doctoral research should be "theory-rich"—based on strong theoretical frameworks that are used to understand and challenge current practices in schools.

Their framework highlights case study methodologies (rather than emphasizing action or intervention approaches). The emphasis is on understanding educational problems in depth by applying academic knowledge to practice as well as on recognizing knowledge that comes from skilled leadership practice. Lochmiller and Lester imagine new opportunities for leaders to "grow in their role as applied researchers" who learn about educational issues through doctoral research training.

Resources for Action Research Dissertation Writers

There are several rich resources for supporting students in educational leadership programs doing some form of action research. Herr and Anderson (2005, 2015) have authored two editions of a comprehensive guide for graduate students and professors of leadership called *The Action Research Dissertation.* In their 2014 edition, the authors trace the multiple traditions of action research, explore issues related to legitimizing and delegitimizing action research in the academy, attend to the construction of action research dissertation proposals, provide several compelling examples, and consider the ethical issues entailed in doing this kind of scholarship.

The authors argue that in addition to valuing and producing local knowledge, this work can also inform the knowledge bases of various fields—and, to that end, encourage graduate students to take their work public through efforts at publication. While not positioned exclusively for doctoral students in leadership programs, these volumes provide thoughtful and provocative perspectives on ways that dissertation research in this vein can make a very valuable contribution to what we know and need to know about leadership practice.

Principal Professional Development as Action Research

While most of the existing literature is concerned with assumptions and practices of doctoral programs and the design of dissertations, Dana (2009) has been focusing on a different genre: the design and enactment of professional development programs and institutes for leaders (new and experienced principals) that teach and guide them in doing action research. In her 2009 methods textbook entitled *Learning with Passion and Knowledge: The Principal as Action Researcher,* Dana defines administrator inquiry as a form of action research distinct from traditional educational research.

Intended for an audience of new and experienced principals, students in higher education and their faculty advisors, and superintendents and other district leaders who organize professional development for principals, Dana's book is the first explicitly focused on principals' roles in action research and her intent is to offer practical tools and rich examples. Dana and her colleagues (Dana, Tricarico, & Quinn, 2009; Dana, Marrs-Morford, & Roberts, 2015) have also conducted case study research on action research for principals as a form of professional development. Dana, Tricarico, and Quinn (2009), for example, found that high-stakes testing environments and accountability mandates shaped principals' inquiries and their understandings of the processes of inquiry in significant ways. In addition, they found that the collaborations of principals significantly informed their understandings of action research as well as their own practice as administrators, and thus enhanced what they knew about school and administrative practice more broadly.

Generating Knowledge from Sites of Practice

While the literature on leadership and inquiry deals primarily with the nature of doctoral education and district-based professional development for leaders, there has also been attention to the possibilities and consequences for individual leaders of engaging in site-based research. In "Knowledge Generation from the Inside Out: The Promise and Perils of Site-Based Research," Anderson and Jones (2000) report on their exploratory study of the potential for educational administrators to generate knowledge out of their own practice settings, arguing that insider research represents a "powerful lever" for personal, professional, and organizational transformation (p. 428). Drawing from published work, dissertation abstracts, and interviews with administrators that represent an explicit effort to generate both *local* and *public* knowledge (see also Cochran-Smith & Lytle, 1993), they provide descriptions of the various topics leaders studied, the methods they used, and some of the practical, epistemological, and political dilemmas they encountered.

Collecting published research-based work authored by administrators is complicated, they argue, not only by its relative scarcity but also because of the "fine line" between administrator narratives and data-based studies. Arguing that research by practitioners presents challenges to the existing forms of knowledge, Anderson and Jones also contend that action research makes problematic the very idea that research has "findings" in the traditional sense of that word. Rather, they point to the great potential of research that foregrounds the leader's practice and potential for knowledge generation from practice.

Drawing from the work of Habermas (1971), who argued that "knowledge production is never neutral but is always pursued with some interest in mind" (p. 449), Anderson and Jones (2000) identify what they see as dilemmas of administrator research, such as possible bias, prejudice, or other unexamined assumptions that need to be acknowledged and scrutinized, including confusion between administrator and research roles. The findings of their study also suggest the political and ethical dilemmas for both the researcher and the researched that can result from leader "truth telling" that yields unintended consequences or the "threat of political controversy." Nevertheless, Anderson and Jones "insist that it is time to begin to take this work seriously as a new source of knowledge with the potential to create powerful cultures of inquiry that promote individual, organizational, and social transformation" (p. 457). Additionally, they argue that "rigorous accounts by administrators that shed light on how administrators frame problems, engage in day-to-day practice, and achieve outcomes informed by data are rare" (p. 434). Their examination of dissertations written by administrators lead them to the conclusion that their "findings reflect deeper understandings of practice, the acknowledgement of new dilemmas and contradictions, gaps between espoused theories and theories-in-use, new self-understandings, or new, more complex questions" (p. 437).

In a more recent article, Anderson and Herr (2009) argue that "educational administrators who are willing to interrogate their own professional practices via practitioner action research can set the climate in their own settings for systemic inquiry that informs locally and beyond" (p. 155). They point out that:

> Administrators doing action research may also have to decide how comfortable they are with controversy, as action research often makes visible those dark corners of the organization in which power and privilege hide. Tracking practices by race or class, excessive referrals of students of color to special education, more access by low-income students to military recruiters than to college recruiters and a plethora of other unethical practices often go unchallenged but could be taken up in action research. (p. 164)

As Zeichner (2001) has observed about practitioner (teacher) research, what practitioners learn from research about their institutions and, in this case, their experiences trying to lead in ways that are contextually meaningful, should not be regarded as merely extending the current knowledge base but also as a challenge to existing assumptions and forms of knowledge.

Leader-Authored Accounts of Inquiry/Research

An important issue in the literature of leadership and inquiry is the scarcity of articles, chapters, or books actually *written by field-based educational leaders* focused on inquiry in one of its myriad forms. There are very few books, for example, authored by practitioner/leaders that provide what Anderson and Jones (2000) describe as "rigorous accounts . . . that shed light on how administrators frame problems, engage in day-to-day practice, and achieve outcomes informed by data" (p. 434).

Although many doctoral programs in educational leadership support action research dissertations, there are relatively few books or edited collections focusing on leader inquiry written by practicing leaders. A recent exception is *Working for Kids: Educational Leadership as Inquiry and Invention,* authored by one of the editors of this book (J. H. Lytle, 2010). The book provides an example of an administrator who in a variety of leadership roles—principal, district research director, and superintendent—tried to lead from an inquiry stance. Lytle writes about his work *as an inquiry.* Rather than simply implementing top-down policies, he explored the local knowledge held within the diverse communities he led and was intentional about how he collaborated with the multiple key stakeholders—those who were closest to the problems—in order to generate a deeper understanding of the issues and possible solutions. Lytle has also published a series of articles about his field-based experiences both doing and promoting inquiry with and among colleagues as a form of field-based leadership development (see, for example, J. H. Lytle, 1996; for another practitioner piece, see also Dinkins, 2009).

Insofar as practitioners in any field have traditionally been assumed to be primarily the objects of research and receivers of knowledge from the university, recent writing about practitioner research suggests that the movement to generate knowledge by practitioners who are currently educational leaders holds promise not only for the leaders themselves, but also for the field more broadly. The prevailing top-down, policy-driven, prescriptive approaches to educational leader training and development, licensure, supervision, and evaluation are inadequate, in that they are not sufficiently informed by field-based knowledge and practice. Furthermore, it seems that many of the most salient and challenging problems of leadership practice are not currently posed or explored in the literature.

Reviewing these published accounts that link leadership and inquiry, we detect obvious resonances with the concept of leading from an inquiry stance: for example, the infusion of organizational learning communities into doctoral programs, an orientation toward participatory forms of research, the desire to join academics and practitioners in newly constituted communities of inquiry, the belief in the importance of what leaders bring to programs and the value of their inquiring into local problems of practice, the potential for engaging in practitioner inquiry as professional development, and perhaps most obvious, the significant possibilities inherent in generating knowledge from sites of leadership practice. In various ways, the authors suggest that efforts to link leadership and inquiry may create new forms of knowledge-making that have the power to challenge what we know about the practice of educational leadership.

REVISITING THE CONCEPT OF LEADING FROM AN INQUIRY STANCE

So how is leading from an inquiry stance a repositioning of educational leadership and different from current conceptions of leadership? As the chapters will clarify, this does not simply equate to "doing an inquiry" (or a dissertation) as an isolated, occasional activity. What we are grappling with is how the concept and practice of *leadership* looks fundamentally different when infused with the stance of inquiry as a powerful habit of mind and a way of "knowing and being" that extends across professional careers and into a range of contexts. As discussed in the previous section, Penn's Mid-Career Doctoral Program provides a range of contexts and opportunities for exploring practitioner research, both individually and in communities of inquiry carved out from the shared interests of colleagues.

The ongoing focus on practitioner research in this program is conceptualized as an approach to helping educational leaders understand the value and implications of adopting an inquiry stance in their practice. Further, it is viewed as a framework in which they can learn how to enact leadership in ways that are driven by data sources that they generate from questions and concerns emerging directly from their practices and settings. While not constructed as reports of their dissertation research per se, seven of the 11 chapters in this volume are written by leaders whose dissertations are the sources of their narratives of an inquiry-based leadership stance.

Though none of the chapters is a traditional report of research, we believe that these varied narratives about inquiry-driven leadership could be considered something of a new genre with the potential to make a significant contribution to the professional literature—partially through the problems posed, but also from the systematic effort to mine site-based data as an aspect of leading, and to describe and analyze the process of doing so. The chapters sit on that "fine line" alluded to by Anderson and Jones (2000) above; all the narratives are informed by data, but what counts as data varies widely, depending on the context and the problem posed.

In summary, leading from an inquiry stance does not submit easily to a single definition; it is a work in progress. It is more than "doing research on their own practice," as authors take up school and system-based issues that encompass the practices of many players. It is about embracing an inquiry stance *as an approach to leading*—and the book provides examples of a range of inquiries by differently positioned leaders. The book is not about a research method or methodology, not simply reflective practice, not self-study. The chapters that follow feature questions posed by differently situated leaders and describe how they have explored the ways these questions significantly inform their work and the work of others.

As editors, co-constructing this volume has meant embracing new learning and new forms of collaboration with mid-career educational leaders who were willing to write about their work. The authors focus on local contexts but also—implicitly or explicitly—grapple with and problematize the broader frames in which they work. We think they point to the myriad ways shared communities of leaders, academic researchers, and program alumni can catalyze a re-thinking of the notion of a knowledge base in educational leadership.

DESIGN OF THE BOOK

The chapters are organized into three sections: Learning from and with Students, Collaborating with Teachers and the School Community, and Leading System-Level Inquiry.

Learning from and with Students

Chapter 1, Melinda Bihn: How do we understand the particular worlds of international students who live between two cultures?
Chapter 2, Ann Dealy: How do we make sense of the lived experiences of public elementary students across multiple languages in and out of school?
Chapter 3, Martha Richmond: What does it mean to rethink "taken-for-granted" school practices that may influence learning opportunities for students and shape the culture of the institution?
Chapter 4, Peter Horn: In what ways might we leverage technology challenges to provide opportunities for student participation and leadership?

Collaborating with Teachers and the School Community

Chapter 5, Patricia Cruice: How do we speak about students to each other? How can we speak about them differently to know them better?
Chapter 6, Noah Tennant: How do we deal with the conflicting cultural realities of those in our school community?
Chapter 7, Kristin Ross Cully: How do we make visible peoples' experiences of what has been a silent aspect of community life at our school?

Leading System-Level Inquiry

Chapter 8, David Trautenberg: What does it mean to learn your way into another professional culture?
Chapter 9, Amy Maisterra: How do we understand and change the bureaucratic inertia of the central office?
Chapter 10, Marquitta Speller: How do we challenge our own assumptions about how we prepare students to be successful?
Chapter 11, Stephen Benson: How does an outsider hold difficult conversations with the local community?

These chapters provide rare windows into how practitioners construct meaning through inquiry into richly contextualized challenges. Not written as "victory stories," the narratives demonstrate some of the power, rigor, and relevance of leading from an inquiry stance.

In the appendices, we offer a description of the Mid-Career Doctoral Program in Educational Leadership as well as a framework for *reading* the texts of leader practitioner inquiry and for *writing* one's own leadership narrative.

REFERENCES

Anderson, G. L., & Herr, K. (1999). The new paradigm wars: Is there room for rigorous practitioner knowledge in schools and universities? *Educational Researcher, 28*(5), pp. 12–21.

Anderson, G. L., & Herr, K. (2009). Practitioner action research and educational leadership. In S. Noffke & B. Somekh (Eds.), *The SAGE handbook of educational action research* (pp. 155–165). Thousand Oaks, CA: SAGE.

Anderson, G. L., Herr, K., & Nihlen, A. S. (1994). *Studying your own school: An educator's guide to qualitative practitioner research*. Thousand Oaks, CA: Corwin.

Anderson, G. L., Herr, K., & Nihlen, A. S. (2007). *Studying your own school: An educator's guide to qualitative practitioner research* (2nd ed.). Thousand Oaks, CA: Corwin.

Anderson, G. L., & Jones, F. (2000). Knowledge generation in educational administration from the inside out: The promise and perils of site-based, administrative research. *Educational Administration Quarterly, 36*(3), 428–464.

Bryk, A. S., Sebring, P. B., Allensworth, E., Luppescu, S., & Easton, J. Q. (2010). *Organizing schools for improvement: Lessons from Chicago*. Chicago, IL: University of Chicago.

Cochran-Smith, M., & Lytle, S. L. (1993). *Inside outside: Teacher research and knowledge*. New York, NY: Teachers College Press.

Cochran-Smith, M., & Lytle, S. L. (2004). Practitioner inquiry, knowledge, and university culture. In J. Loughran, M. L. Hamilton, V. LaBoskey, & T. Russell (Eds.), *International handbook of research of self-study of teaching and teacher education practices* (pp. 601–650). London, United Kingdom: Kluwer Publishers.

Cochran-Smith, M., & Lytle, S. L. (2009). *Inquiry as stance: Practitioner research for the next generation*. New York, NY: Teachers College Press.

Dana, N. F. (2009). *Leading with passion and knowledge: The principal as action researcher*. Thousand Oaks, CA: Corwin and American Association of School Administrators.

Dana, N. F., Marrs-Morford, L., & Roberts, S. (2015). The promise of action research: Lessons learned from the Indiana Principal Leadership Institute. *LEARNing Landscape, 9*(1), 59–79.

Dana, N., Tricarico, K., & Quinn, D. M. (2009) The administrator as action researcher: A case study of five principals and their engagement in systematic, intentional study of their own practice. *Journal of School Leadership, 9*(1), 232–265.

Dinkins, D. (2009). Teachers talk about race, class, and achievement. In M. Cochran-Smith & S. L. Lytle (Eds.), *Inquiry as stance* (pp. 254–274). New York, NY: Teachers College Press.

Donmoyer, R. (1999). The continuing quest for a knowledge base: 1976–1998. In J. Murphy & K. S. Louis (Eds.), *Handbook of research on educational administration,* 2nd ed. (pp. 23–44). San Francisco, CA: Jossey-Bass.

Freire, P. (1970). *Pedagogy of the oppressed.* New York, NY: Continuum.

Greene, M. (2000). *Releasing the imagination: Essays in education, the arts, and social change.* San Francisco, CA: Jossey-Bass. (Original work published 1995)

Habermas, J. (1971). *Knowledge and human interests.* Boston, MA: Beacon.

Heifetz, R. A., & Linsky, M. (2002). *Leadership on the line: Staying alive through the dangers of leading.* Cambridge, MA: Harvard Business School.

Herr, K., & Anderson, G. L. (2005). *The action research dissertation: A guide for students and faculty.* Thousand Oaks, CA: SAGE.

Herr, K., & Anderson, G. L. (2015). *The action research dissertation: A guide for students and faculty.* (2nd ed.). Thousand Oaks, CA: SAGE.

Lochmiller, C. R., & Lester, J. N. (2017). Conceptualizing practitioner-scholarship for educational leadership research and practice. *Journal of Research on Leadership Education, 12*(1), 3–25.

Lytle, J. H. (1996). The inquiring manager: Developing new structures to support reform. *Phi Delta Kappan, 77*(10), 664–670.

Lytle, J. H. (2010). *Working for kids: Education leadership as inquiry and invention.* Latham, MD: Rowman & Littlefield.

Lytle, J. H., & Sokoloff, H. J. (2013). A complex web: The new normal for superintendents. *School Administrator 70*(8), 21–25.

McCarthy, Y. (2014). Reflections presented at the first Leading from an Inquiry Stance Writing Retreat, July 2014, Philadelphia, PA.

Morgan, G. (1997). *Images of organization* (2nd ed.). Thousand Oaks, CA: Sage.

Noffke, S., & Somekh, B. (Eds.) (2009). *The SAGE handbook of educational action research.* Thousand Oaks, CA: SAGE.

Osterman, K., Furman, G., & Sernak, K. (2014). Action research in EdD Programs in educational leadership. *Journal of Research on Leadership Education, 9*(1), 85–105.

Reason, P., & Bradbury, H. (2001). *Handbook of action research: Participative inquiry and practice.* Thousand Oaks: SAGE

Riehl, C., Larson, C. L., Short., P. M., & Reitzug, U. C. (2000). Reconceptualizing research and scholarship in educational administration: Learning to know, knowing to do, doing to learn. *Educational Administration Quarterly, 36*(30), 391–427.

Sargut, G., & McGrath, R. (2011). Learning to live with complexity. *Harvard Business Review. 89*(9), 68–76.

Wahlstrom, K. L., Seashore-Lewis, K., Leithwood, K., & Anderson, S. E. (2010). *Investigating the links to improved student learning: Executive Summary of research findings [and] Final report of research findings.* New York, NY: The Wallace Foundation.

Zeichner, K. (2001). Educational action research. In P. Reason & H. Bradbury (Eds.), *Handbook of action research: Participative inquiry and practice* (pp. 273–283). Thousand Oaks, CA: Sage.

Part I

LEARNING FROM AND WITH STUDENTS

CHAPTER 1

Inquiring to Lead

Learning With, From, and About International Students in Independent Schools

Melinda Bihn

Melinda Bihn is the head of school at French American International School and International High School in San Francisco, California. She has been a teacher of English and an administrator in international schools in Europe and independent schools in the United States. Bihn's dissertation explored the experiences of unaccompanied international students in a U.S. independent school where she served as Head of Upper School. She earned her doctorate in education from the University of Pennsylvania, a master's degree in the teaching and administration of English as a second language from Trenton State College (overseas), a master's in comparative literature from the University of North Carolina at Chapel Hill, and her bachelor's degree from Santa Clara University.

Independent schools are a small subset of U.S. schools, and international students in independent schools are a small group within that world. But the challenge of understanding and supporting students of different backgrounds is familiar to every school leader; central to good leadership in any school is ensuring that it is a just and equitable place for all students, and especially for those who may not feel entirely at home in the school's culture. This is the story of how I inquired into international students' experiences in my independent school, and of how that inquiry transformed my leadership practice. Rather than presenting my leadership of a single initiative, this chapter describes the sequence of inquiries I undertook as a school leader and doctoral student and the resulting evolution of my leadership. It is a narrative of learning with and about students, and also of learning how to lead—a description of how inquiry with students and on behalf of students has transformed my understanding of questions of consequence in my school and also my practice of leadership. In these pages, I discuss an initial inquiry, undertaken as a teaching principal, into my students' understanding of social identity and experience of diversity. I then focus on the experience of international students, as well as a faculty inquiry to which that initial project led. Finally, I reflect on the ways the practice of inquiry transformed my leadership as a principal and informs my leadership as a Head of School in an independent international school.

CONTEXT AND PROBLEM-POSING

The Woodland School (TWS)* is an independent, pre-K-to-12th-grade, U.S. day and boarding school for girls, which prides itself on its long-standing commitment to the education of young women and on the diversity of its student body. The school's historical commitment to meeting the needs of the individual girl has been matched, in recent decades, by deliberate efforts to include in the school community groups historically marginalized or excluded from independent education. The result is a student body that is diverse in terms of socioeconomic status, sexual orientation, race, and religion. During my time there, one third of high school students were students of color, including a relatively small but financially significant population of 36 international boarding students, most of whom came to the school from China and Korea. While the school had long welcomed some international boarders, their numbers had recently grown as TWS, like many U.S. independent schools, looked to international students to strengthen its enrollment, especially in the wake of the 2008 recession.

As a principal, I was drawn to the school by its commitment to diversity, which is underscored by its mission statement, motto, and slogan, and I proudly spoke of this commitment in my communications about the school. Nonetheless, the school's history and culture, like those of many U.S. independent schools, occur in the context of an exclusive educational experience, access to which was until relatively recently restricted by class, race, and religion and framed by an assumption of American citizenship. The school still retains many of the markers of a culture of whiteness and privilege that characterize most independent schools, as much of the research on diversity and independent education suggests (see, for example, Gaztambide-Fernández & DiAquoi, 2010). Educators know the power of cultural context in students' experience of school and how a mismatch can undermine the educational enterprise. In my role as principal, understanding how students experienced their social identities in the school was important to ensuring that TWS provided an equitable environment for all students.

That I was also teaching English literature to a group of 12th-graders gave extra impetus to my desire to learn more about our students. Daily, I was a classroom witness to the girls' sense-making of their school experience, and I saw the potential disjunction between the promise and the reality of diversity in the independent school context. Snatches of overheard conversation, seating patterns in class, and the relative silences of our international students, in particular, made me wonder about students' lived experience of their social identities at TWS. I brought these questions to my studies at the University of Pennsylvania. A student

*The name of the school has been changed. All student names are pseudonyms.

myself, I wanted to learn with and from—not just about—the students I served; my reading in critical race theory (Delgado & Stefancic, 2012) had shown me the importance of foregrounding students' voices in research about them. "Why not do an inquiry?" suggested a professor during my first year of doctoral study, when I described the kind of research that interested me. Thus began a process of learning with my students and colleagues that transformed both my research and my leadership practice.

LEARNING TO INQUIRE: IN THE CLASSROOM

The class reflected the diversity of the high school: Of 16 students, six were international; six were non-native speakers of English; and nine were students of color. A good literature class, as English teachers know, is as much "about" the students as it is about the texts studied. The senior English curriculum, the second semester of which focused on identity themes in canonical and contemporary texts, offered an ideal context in which to explore questions of identity and school culture.

My students and I read Sophocles's *Oedipus Rex*, a collection of poems exploring family relationships and social identity, and Marion Winik's lively memoir, *Rules for the Unruly*, and we took part in literature circles on additional memoirs. In personal and analytical writing, class discussions, and writing conferences, the girls explored their understanding of their own identities and reflected on their experience in school. Activities and assignments included free writes, journal entries, creative pieces, a book review, a memoir of school, and literary essays. Attending to students' stories and meaning-making, I took notes during discussions and conferences and kept a teaching journal. The emphasis in this project on students' views reflects the tenets of critical race theory, which privileges individual voices and attends to their stories, as well as intersectionality theory, which acknowledges the many and multiple forces that shape participants' identity and experience (Zuberi & Bonilla-Silva, 2008). As I built inquiry into the structure of the class, my teaching practice deepened; I adopted a critical pedagogy that foregrounded the voices of my students.

In response, they told powerful stories about the ways they understood themselves and made meaning of their experience in school. While the girls differed in significant ways, their stories revealed shared understandings and actions, and from the stories several themes emerged. The girls saw identity differently than I did, resisting categories I had not questioned. They made choices about their identities, selecting among the aspects of identity available to them—especially race, gender, class, and nationality. This move allowed them to "talk back" to categories that they perceived as imposed on them and that I had initially imposed on my thinking. As they asserted their ability and right to decide for themselves who they were and how they would be defined, they constructed counter-stories of highly individual, evolving understandings of themselves.

These choices among social identities were narrative acts of affiliation and resistance through which the students insisted on their autonomy, but which also revealed the power of social identity in their lives. In their writing and discussions, the girls wrestled with the fixed identity framework they encountered in the world around them, aligning themselves with or distinguishing themselves from racial, socioeconomic, religious, and national groups with varying degrees of success. School often constituted a threat to their sense of social identity, and the international students in the class found it especially challenging to sustain their sense of social identity and to navigate school culture effectively. In their writing and in conferences, they spoke powerfully of the differences between the cultures of home and school and of the ways they were changing in response to their experiences of both. They described feeling isolated from their American classmates and distant from their families as they faced the challenges of living and studying abroad. Their stories were moving—and sometimes difficult for me, as their teacher and principal, to hear.

Two moments compelled me to learn more about the ways that international students, in particular, were shaped by their time in our school. While describing her experience of a history class at TWS, one of the international students noted that when the teacher "says 'we' in class, she means the United States. That's so interesting, and it makes sense." She paused for a moment and then looked steadily at me as she added, "But I am not part of that 'we.'" As a principal and a teacher, I was struck by the way Tamara positioned herself within the school yet outside its community. The sense of displacement she described with the phrase "I am not part of that 'we'" stayed with me long afterward, as I considered the complex accommodations and affiliations that contributed to the experiences of our international students. I began to wonder what belonging meant to these students and what it might take to make them part of the school's "we."

The second moment was equally powerful and more deeply distressing. During a writing conference, another international student talked passionately about applying to the Ivy League schools that were meaningful to her family and friends in China. However, as a member of an over-represented group in the applicant pool, she met with general rejection from these schools despite her exemplary academic achievement. Qin spoke of what she had learned from the process and what we might learn from her experience at TWS. At the end of the conversation, I asked her what advice she would give to another student from China—and, suddenly, she was crying. She made no sound, but the tears rolled steadily down her cheeks; her hair fell forward, curtaining the sides of her face. "I would tell her that it's just—that it's just that—that it's just that there are rules, and you have to follow the rules, and even if you do you won't get what you want and you work for—because you are Chinese," she said in a rush, never looking up. In that moment, as she wept with frustration and disappointment, I was overwhelmed with concern for this young woman, so far from her home and so alone in her sadness, and I had a glimpse of what was at stake for our international students, who bring not just their own dreams but also their families' hopes to their education in a new country.

As a teacher and a principal, I was deeply troubled by these conversations. They challenged me because in my role as high school principal, I was responsible not only for the learning but also for the well-being of the nearly 300 students in our division of the school. I was concerned about the experiences that Tamara, Qin, and other international students described, and I was also intrigued by the ways in which they described them. I had experienced international life myself; 10 years as a young teacher in international schools in Austria, Germany, and Portugal had shaped both my sense of identity and my practice as a teacher and school leader, and I knew that living in other countries and cultures had marked me indelibly. Yet my experiences as a young adult abroad were inadequate for making sense of my students': They had traveled farther than I ever had, at a much younger age, in pursuit of an education whose implications it was suddenly clear I did not fully understand.

INQUIRING TO LEARN: INTERNATIONAL STUDENTS IN AN INDEPENDENT SCHOOL

Inquiry aims for "a profound change, a paradigm shift, a different direction in terms of purposes and aims, with the ultimate goal of enhancing students' learning and their life chances" (Cochran-Smith & Lytle, 2009, p. 147). As a teaching principal, I had undertaken an inquiry in order to deepen my understanding of my students. What I learned changed the way I saw them, my school, and myself, and now I found myself adopting an inquiry stance as a leader. I needed to know more in order to address what I had learned. And I discovered that, in 2012, the topic of international students in independent schools was largely unresearched. Therefore, I designed my dissertation study as an inquiry with international students around how they understood and experienced their social identities in our school, how they perceived our school culture, and how they navigated the school environment in light of their identities and experiences.

In this sustained inquiry, I drew on several literatures and critical theories to learn how to listen to the voices of international students and to understand their lived experience in our school. My initial classroom-based inquiry had confirmed for me the power of critical race and intersectionality theories as theoretical frames for this work and revealed a need for a theory of resistance in understanding the stories it uncovered. In this next project, I again sought to foreground students' voices, giving place to their stories, and engaging their knowledge while listening for the intersection and interplay of forces—of nationality, race, gender, and class—at work in their lives. This theoretical approach informed my choice of methods as well. As in the earlier inquiry, I placed myself in a position of learning from my students rather than simply about them, situating this project in my practice as a principal and thus in the tradition of practitioner research described by Cochran-Smith and Lytle (2009) and Anderson, Herr, and Nihlen (1994, 2007).

In this inquiry, I worked collaboratively with 17 11th- and 12th-grade international students and four recent international alumnae. I interviewed alums on the telephone and spoke with each current student in person, opening each meeting with an invitation to draw an identity map—that is, to create an image of the experience of being an international student. I also held two focus group conversations for current students, many of whom chose to participate. The encounters were sequenced so that questions that arose from student interviews could be taken up in the focus groups, and so that conversations with international alumnae could be used to check initial impressions from my conversations with current students.

This work was more complex than the earlier classroom inquiry. As a principal, I needed to mitigate the power of my role in these encounters, particularly for current students: It was possible, even in a collaborative inquiry, that students and or alumnae would feel uneasy about sharing their experience or opinions with me. By sharing information with participants and their parents about the nature and purpose of the study, I built a sense of trust in the inquiry; the students were universally appreciative of my interest in their experience and willing to talk with me. In order to address any concerns that might nonetheless arise, I secured permission for the project from our Head of School and identified a colleague, the Dean of Students, as a person to whom students and parents could bring questions or concerns (and thus remain anonymous to me) if they did not wish to make me aware of these directly. Additionally, students and I met in a space outside my office (which was often the site of parent meetings and occasionally the location of disciplinary conversations). Instead, we spoke in a public space in a non-academic building outside our section of the school.

Despite the challenges inherent in my role, there were also strengths that resulted from it. As Anderson, Herr, and Nihlen (2007) note in relation to action research, this kind of work "has the potential for empowerment and the inclusion of a greater diversity of voices in educational policy and social change" (p. 7). My position made this inquiry possible, and throughout it, students told me what it meant to them that I was taking a rigorous look at their experience. My attention to them, in my role as principal, affirmed their importance in our school community. "I actually appreciate the chance, that you want us to talk," said Fei, while Zhixiao noted, "I want to say one more time thank you for taking your time, also, to get to know our feelings and our life." Their sentiments were echoed by every student and alumna with whom I spoke, all of whom thanked me for the inquiry, as did their families. My dual role as a researcher and school leader also positioned me to conduct a larger professional conversation about these students in our school. Later in this chapter, I discuss the additional inquiry that I undertook with the faculty.

Thus, I came to spend a long series of late afternoons on the sun porch with my students, watching the sun set behind school buildings as the girls drew striking images on their maps, listening closely as they told, at first hesitantly and then with a growing sense of urgency, stories of what it meant to cross the world alone and come to our school. The conversations affected me profoundly. The girls drew maps of their experience that were almost always divided between home and here, with a line between the images that revealed, as Zhen described it, "the invisible line in my heart." They spoke of their journeys across the world and their experiences on our campus, of the effects of these experiences on their sense of self, and of the ways they sought relationships and constructed communities at our school. They explained the changes that took place within themselves and in their families as a result of their international experience, and they explored its meaning for their futures.

Again, their stories were not entirely easy to hear. The girls spoke with appreciation about aspects of their time at TWS and with affection about the school community, their teachers especially; they were all grateful for the educational experience afforded them by their study abroad. But many of their stories ran counter to the school's mission and values, especially our avowed commitment at TWS to diversity and equity. It was difficult to hear stories that suggested institutional misunderstanding, and even bias, from students about whom my colleagues and I cared and whom we sought to support and serve. Yet these counter-stories, however painful to hear, were vital to my learning and, ultimately, to my leadership.

What I learned, as I listened, is that our international students experienced a divided sense of self as a result of their transnational education, and that they responded to this by deliberately constructing new identities that incorporated their home cultures as well as their experiences abroad. Similarly, in reaction to the distance from families and friends at home and from their U.S. peers at school, they deliberately created national communities of shared support that allowed them to resist assimilation. Finally, in the context of a school culture that presented problems for them in many of its practices and policies, and that problematized them as a result, they often had to forgo belonging in order to facilitate achievement and thus fulfill the expectations of their international academic experience.

As I sought to understand the girls' stories and their meaning for our school, I found myself developing a deeper understanding of our independent school culture and of independent education itself. While this study highlighted uncomfortable issues in our school, in ways that were often challenging for me, it also raised important ones for independent education, and it did so in a way that honored the mission and educational ethos of our school. The theme of racialized nationality ran through the girls' descriptions of their intersecting identities and their experiences of home and school; the girls' narratives present a powerful challenge to the norms of whiteness and American-ness in the dormitories and dining halls, classrooms and curricula of independent schools. Stories of their school experiences revealed, for example, that in our school, international students did not own aspects of the school culture—the holiday calendar, the dining hall menu, and the academic curriculum, for instance—the way that their U.S. peers did. The terms of the transnational educational experience—academic achievement, leading to excellence in college acceptance—placed them at odds with some of the academic policies and practices of the independent school. For example, policies that made mastery of English the prime measure of academic ability (and served as the basis for placement in courses) created barriers to the students' goals of high achievement.

The counter-stories of these international students also revealed how the norm of racialized nationality obscured other aspects of their identities. The girls insisted on the complexity of their identities, in which not only nationality and race but also language, gender, and class were at work, and thus spoke back to a school culture that, in their experience, viewed them as simply Asian and foreign. Their stories suggest little awareness in the independent school setting of either the rich intersectionality of international students' identities or the real challenges of their experience in our schools.

INQUIRING TO LEAD: WITH THE FACULTY

What I learned also challenged my leadership, since many of the stories the girls shared ran counter to the ideas of inclusion and access that ground not only my values as an educator but also the school's values as an institution. As my work on this inquiry deepened, I grew increasingly concerned about, and yet committed to, sharing my learning with my colleagues. I knew that what I was learning would challenge the teachers' understanding of our school and of themselves, and I also knew that without my colleagues' buy-in, our students' experience could not be improved.

During the course of this inquiry, I saw proof of the challenges the girls described: There were teacher requests to place ESL students below grade level, for example, and the course selection process erupted in conflict when, despite strong grades and PSAT scores, many international students initially found themselves denied access to Advanced Placement courses because of a perceived lack of adequate English. Faculty comments reflected unease with the growing number of international students on campus. While the school's and international students' interests converged around the girls' enrollment at TWS—meeting the school's need for financial sustainability by fulfilling international families' desire for transnational education—these interests had clearly not yet aligned within the academic curriculum and school culture. Perceiving international students as an answer to a financial problem, some faculty members seemed to see them as a challenge to the school's program.

I had learned through my experience of inquiry thus far that I would need to inquire with my colleagues about their experience of teaching international students, rather than simply tell them what I had learned. In a sequence of faculty meetings, I conducted a mini-inquiry with the high school faculty into how they experienced their work with international students. Using peer interviews, which mitigated the difficulties posed by my supervisory role, we considered the challenges and rewards in that work, and reflected on how the school shaped their experience of international students. Having teachers interview each other positioned them as equal partners with me in the inquiry and contributed to trust in the conversations. In a subsequent meeting, I shared emerging themes from these interviews and asked in a focus group how our school and its leadership might improve that experience. Finally, I invited individual communications from my colleagues, in case they had additional thoughts they preferred to share privately.

This mini-inquiry deepened my understanding of the context in which our international students' narratives cohered: What I learned was that the rapid growth of this group of students and the challenge of teaching them constituted a kind of culture shock for the high school faculty, who were moving both individually and collectively through predictable stages of that experience. Most of my colleagues admired our international students and valued their contributions to the school community. They sought to integrate international students into the school community and struggled with the challenges posed by this. They needed more information about international students, more knowledge of the girls' home cultures and experience at school, and more support of their work with these students. What I had seen as a problem with teachers' responses to students from other cultures was, upon inquiry, more accurately viewed as a response from teachers to changes in our own.

This inquiry not only provided me with insight into my colleagues' thinking but also reoriented my leadership toward empathy with teachers in the service of equity for students. I had been frustrated by reactions to these students, but I had not inquired into teachers' experience of working with them. My understanding of my colleagues had been grounded in my reaction to their behavior rather than in an understanding of their experience. Inquiring into their experience, as I had into the experience of our students, invited me to lead with understanding, and it allowed me to consider what had seemed an individual problem or an intergroup conflict at the level of organizational dynamics. This inquiry thus presented an opportunity not only to shape our faculty's thinking but also to reframe my own.

It was in particular an opportunity to reframe my thinking about leadership—to see inquiry as a way of leading, rather than simply as a research or even teaching method, and to focus my leadership on working with my colleagues to address the challenges that require the best thinking of entire school communities. It extended my thinking about critical practice in education from the relationship between teacher and student to the relationship between school leaders and teachers, revealing the importance of listening to teachers' voices as well.

Inquiry, I discovered, is a powerful tool in both research and leadership. It is also catching. While I was working on these projects, I was approached by a group of faculty of color about their experiences on campus. My response was informed by my growing experience of inquiry: On the same sun porch where I had spent hours with my students, I listened to my colleagues' stories and concerns and then, swallowing all my instincts to explain and assuage, asked them what they thought we should do—and how I could support that work. They proposed a faculty research grant into issues of equity and inclusion, which we funded and which led to professional development for faculty and staff. Inquiring leadership, I realized, leads to inquiry and learning throughout the school.

CONCLUSIONS: ACTIONS AND UNDERSTANDINGS

In this chapter, I have described a sequence of inquiries—in the classroom, on the campus, and among the faculty—that arose from and informed my principalship. Because inquiry is practiced with and not on others in our schools, it insists, by its very nature, on action. *What will we do?* arises naturally from *What have we learned?* By the time I began to write my dissertation, we were already doing this work at TWS: We had completed the faculty inquiry and held professional development on international students and language learning, and we were working on several of the issues that our students had identified, including our academic placement process and our communication with international families. As a result of the diversity conversations described above, a small group of faculty was conducting research and planning programming for our students and colleagues.

Inquiry is deeply personal, as well. As I wrote about this inquiry in my dissertation (Bihn, 2014), I was recruited to the headship of an international school. My leaving TWS certainly rendered my research less powerful for my colleagues there. In the context of my upcoming departure, sharing my learning was difficult; it was clear that what our students said about their experience was hard to hear, even when presented in response to the faculty's desire to learn.

The lack of institutional impact of this work during my remaining time at TWS was disappointing to me. Still, in my new role as the head of one of this country's largest international schools, I have found ways to share my learning and to participate in the larger conversation in independent and international schools about diversity and equity. What I had studied with my students and colleagues led me to a discussion in the wider independent school community specifically about international students, to participate in the creation of the National Association of Independent Schools (NAIS) set of Principles of Good Practice for the education of international students, and to share my learning at conferences and in webinars. In that way, I feel that this work has had some effect on the experience of these students, who come so far to learn in our schools.

The greatest effect, however, has been on my own leadership practice. As a leader, I was changed by inquiry: I learned to learn with and from the people I was leading, and I believe that I lead differently now as a result. My new role presents many opportunities to lead by learning. The instincts of inquiry—inclusion of those involved in the problem, respect for their voices regardless of their place in the school hierarchy, acknowledgment of the complexity of their experience—can deeply inform leadership and can make our schools more just and equitable places for all of us who live and learn in them.

REFERENCES

Anderson, G. L., Herr, K., & Nihlen, A. S. (1994, 2007). *Studying your own school: An educator's guide to qualitative practitioner research.* Thousand Oaks, CA: Corwin.

Bihn, M. L. (2014). *"The line in my heart": How international students in a U.S. Independent school conceptualize and experience their social identities* (Doctoral dissertation). Retrieved from ProQuest Dissertations & Theses Database. (UMI No. 3622630).

Cochran-Smith, M., & Lytle, S. L. (2009). *Inquiry as stance: Practitioner research for the next generation*. New York, NY: Teachers College Press.

Delgado, R., & Stefancic, J. (2012). *Critical race theory: An introduction*. New York, NY: New York University Press.

Gaztambide-Fernández, R., & DiAquoi, R. (2010). A part and apart: Students of color negotiating boundaries at an elite boarding school. In R. Gaztambide-Fernández & A. Howard (Eds.), *Educating elites: Class privilege and educational advantage* (pp. 55–77). New York, NY: Rowman & Littlefield Education.

Zuberi, T., & Bonilla-Silva, E. (Eds.). (2008). *White logic, White methods: Racism and methodology*. New York, NY: Rowman & Littlefield Publishers.

CHAPTER 2

Language and Third Spaces

Ann Dealy

Ann Dealy is the principal of Brookside Elementary School in the Ossining Union Free School District located in Westchester County north of New York City. Previously, she served as principal at Park School where she helped to co-found the Dos Voces/Un Mundo (Two Voices/One World) Dual Language Program in 2004. Dealy received her doctorate in educational leadership from the University of Pennsylvania. She earned an advanced certification in leadership from Teachers College, Columbia University; a certification in multicultural and multilingual studies from the College of New Rochelle; a Master of Science degree with concentrations in special education, literacy, and English from the College of Saint Rose; and a Bachelor of Arts in English from the College of New Rochelle.

The day his mother was arrested, high school senior Diego Ismael Puma Macancela, a 19-year-old Ecuadorian, fled to his cousin's apartment. The next day, he cowered with her in a bedroom as U.S. Immigration and Customs Enforcement (ICE) agents pounded on the door. "Wake up," he told his cousin. "The police are here again. They're coming for me." He eventually walked outside and was arrested, hours before his senior prom. "He's not a criminal," his cousin lamented. "He was just going to school, working . . . trying to make his dreams come true for him, for his family, for us. I don't know why [they took him]. He's just a kid." Victoria Gearity, Ossining's mayor, said the arrest played out in front of her. "As people were heading out to work, and kids were walking to the bus stop, three federal agents were walking around the property of the house across the street from me," she told a national newspaper covering story (McKinney & Fitz-Gibbon, 2017).

Eight days later, as Diego sat in a federal detention center pending deportation, seven of his fellow students from Ossining High School and my student partners in this inquiry walked across the stage to receive their diplomas with yellow New York State Seal of Biliteracy cords hanging around their necks. Reflecting on our shared inquiry over the last several years into their linguistic, cultural, and civic development, I looked on with pride. The development of active and culturally conscious citizens of all backgrounds never seemed more important. As a 22-year veteran educator and a resident in the district, I am proud that my granddaughter is part of the same Dos Voces program; the Mayor, whose children also participate, shares my pride. Yet neither of us fears early morning assaults on our door. Diego's story highlighted just how vast the "gap" can be between the experiences of immigrant and native-born students in our community.

Diego's story embodies the complexity of mission and values in my district, its dual language program, and the broader community. Our district's motto advocates "Equity with Excellence," and we claim proudly to "prepare students to become citizens in our American democracy." These values frame the dual language program and its goal of developing bilingual, biliterate, and bicultural citizens. I share these values, and I am profoundly committed to its promise to develop students who can communicate with, understand, and serve all their fellow citizens. Indeed, as I think about the person my granddaughter will grow up to be, it is these values that inform my dreams for her and for the future of Ossining, the special and diverse community where I choose to live and work.

From my early days preparing to be an administrator through my first years as an elementary school principal, my colleagues and I wrestled with issues of race, culture, and language, seeking to make meaning in ways that would serve our students and families well. The historical and demographic context frames and has informed how I have tried to understand my ongoing leadership inquiry in Ossining. After initially responding in fairly conventional ways, my colleagues' and my efforts were enriched as we integrated students into that process, learning in turn a great deal about the dynamics of the "third spaces" in which they live between cultures (García, Makar, Starcevic, & Terry, 2011). We continue to embed this ongoing learning more thoroughly within our district practices.

WAVES NEAR THE RIVER

Just 30 miles north of New York City, the Ossining Union Free School District serves a culturally, linguistically, and economically diverse community with a significant immigrant population. Ossining's 25,000 residents live atop the hills overlooking the picturesque Hudson River, with the Sing-Sing Correctional Facility, the town's largest employer, sitting on its banks.

The demographics of the community have changed considerably in the last 4 decades, and these shifts are reflected in the schools. In 1975, 20 years before my arrival in Ossining, 75% of the 5,136 students in the district were White, 19% were Black, and a mere 5% were Hispanic (Flemming, Horn, Freeman, Ruiz, & Saltzman, 1977). By 2000, 5 years after my arrival, Ossining's Hispanic population had increased more than five times to 28%, while White residents dropped to 60%, and the Black population stayed roughly constant. Some 17 years later, the White population's percentage has shrunk by half to 31%, the Hispanic population makes up nearly half of the residents, and the Black population's percentage has declined by a quarter. Almost 40% of the inhabitants are now foreign-born, largely from Latin America (including a significant Ecuadorian community).

Over the years, the district struggled to respond to the evolving, diversifying community. From 1968 to 1974, Ossining experienced rising racial tensions and disturbances, culminating in a 1974 high school cafeteria fight that eventually spilled out onto the streets downtown. As a result of this melee that injured 19 students, a curfew was established, and unwanted national attention descended on the village. The district finally adopted a variant of the Princeton Plan, organizing schools by grade level rather than neighborhood so each school would reflect the demographics of the overall community. The community celebrated a 20-year "peace" anniversary just before I arrived for the first high school graduates to have attended integrated schools throughout their years in the district (Costello, 1994).

By my arrival, however, the demographics were already shifting dramatically again, toward an increasingly Hispanic community. I have been trying to understand the implications of my role in our learning community ever since. How does one lead schooling and enhance support to a diversifying community, across painful personal and public histories—amidst counter-reactions that include longtime neighbors, many of whom look like me, moving away, while new policies sever families with a knock at the door?

INQUIRING AMONG NEW NEIGHBORS

My story in Ossining began in 1995 as a young special education teacher. During my first interview with the school district, I was drawn to the description of Ossining as home to diverse students similar to New York City's yet with greater resources available to teach them. I was also drawn to the stated value of the district that learning in a diverse school cultivates cultural understanding and appreciation. While I still deeply embrace this value, I continue to learn how complex my students' realities often are.

My transformation of understanding of privilege and systemic inequity began during my leadership studies in the Future School Administrators Academy (FSAA), a partnership between Teachers College, Columbia University, and the Putnam/Northern Westchester Board of Cooperative Educational Services (BOCES). My first professor, Dr. Thomas Sobol, a former New York State Commissioner of Education and a strong equity advocate, interrogated the systems and structures that contribute to the achievement and opportunity gaps for students of color.

Through these academic experiences and with the assistance of my colleagues, my own awareness emerged slowly. I knew so little of my own White privilege. In a moment that stands out, I recall reading and discussing Peggy McIntosh's "Unpacking the White Backpack" with a Black friend and colleague; as she shared her own stories, I began to put real lives into my overly-abstract understanding of the challenges we faced in Ossining. Since then, I have been trying to understand others' experience and locate myself as a White woman in the mission of realizing equity. As my friend and I imagined new directions for Ossining, a White colleague in my cohort urged caution, suggesting that more programs for students of color would only accelerate White flight. His words have echoed in my mind over time as we have expanded such programs and in fact experienced a dramatic decline in our White residents. I have sought to understand the experiences of students of color amidst shifting demographics, as well as the perspectives of some White students that the focus of the district is primarily on serving culturally and linguistically diverse students.

ELEMENTARY RESPONSES

As I inquired into our community's internal divisions and into my own role within it, the district responded in some traditional ways, forming task forces and inviting external eyes into the district. As I approached my graduation from the FSAA program, then superintendent Dr. Robert Roelle convened a group of diverse teachers, administrators, and community members as The Superintendent's Advisory Council on the Achievement Gap. While I was not part of the Advisory Council officially, I was very interested in their work. The Council expressed concerns over the lack of representation of diverse cultures in the curriculum; family reports of poor school climate for "minority" students; low expectations for student achievement; and lack of professional development in diversity, multiculturalism, and language acquisition.

I became an elementary school principal the next year. Uncertain and new, I took a fairly conventional approach. I dedicated two professional staff development sessions monthly to implement the Council's recommendations for a more culturally-responsive education. Though intended as a positive step, it feels rather timid in retrospect, especially given the long history of concerns in the community. Did our unease as professionals make technical solutions more attractive than deeper inquiries? Several years later, as our Spanish-speaking community continued to grow rapidly, we formed yet another committee of teachers and administrators to research and plan a programmatic response. In 2004, we initiated a 50/50 Two-way Immersion (TWI) model at the elementary school, the Dos Voces/ Un Mondo (Two Voices/One World) Dual Language Program. As in other TWI programs, homerooms of students from two language backgrounds (English and Spanish) would rotate daily between instruction in their home and target language and spend an approximately equal amount of time learning in both languages. Eventually, these dual language sections comprised almost 30% of the elementary classes. While still modest as an approach, I was encouraged that we had begun to respond to our students by shifting their classroom experiences.

My attention to culturally- and linguistically-focused professional development continued well through 2007, though the approach to faculty learning evolved over time, nudging our work closer to students' lived experiences. In 2005, we began a relationship with Learner-Centered Initiatives, Ltd., to support our introduction to Collegial Learning Circles to study issues of practice in self-selected groups. Over time, these circles were structured into vertical teams, and topics of study were identified together when looking at students' assessment data. As a result, professional development shifted from looking for answers outside of the school to improve our practice to studying our students as learners and collaborating on changes in practice to better support teaching and learning. We began to open up, tentatively, to questions that surfaced once we brought students' lives beyond our walls into the discussion. Eventually, my teachers and I became accustomed to inquiring about students' backgrounds more regularly, more attentively, and our norms of collective inquiry began to strengthen. Some certainly only saw this all as an effort to gain information, a bit more data in a data-driven world; others, though, saw an opportunity to understand not just our students but ourselves and the community our inquiries could shape.

At the same time, many of my elementary students had passed into the town's secondary school. Also during this period, an external review raised concerns of how my former students were experiencing the high school. The Metropolitan Center for Urban Education used surveys, achievement data, and interviews to explore the student experience at Ossining High School (Noguera, Sealey-Ruiz, Fergus, Christodoulou, Handville, Meade, & Torres, 2007). Amidst varied recommendations to enhance academic opportunities for all students, the report painted a painful picture of the experiences of students of color at the high school. From the in-depth student interview data, I could hear the voices of students whom I knew from their elementary school days. They told of expectations based on their skin color, and of the school's level of concern and care being a function of their immigration status and home language. This hit me like a punch in the stomach. These were the students, and families, to whom we—I perhaps most emphatically—had promised to provide excellence, and to do so equitably. It was a shocking and upsetting read.

What struck me was the need to shift how we as educators received and responded to this powerful narrative. Another task force, more professional development, another program—these weren't going to shift what was now clearly a persistent tension across more than a decade. We, as a community, had a messy, complex challenge that demanded a collective, self-reflective, ongoing inquiry. We needed to speak honestly of our ignorance—first of our students' experiences and second of our own roles within them. To lead such an inquiry, I had to locate myself within this collective challenge. Had my incremental approach reinforced the status quo? Did the programming we implemented actually replicate the inequities we sought to remedy? We needed to open up our inquiry stance further and include more robustly the voices and thinking of our colleagues and students.

STUDENT PARTNERS IN INQUIRY

To delve further, I sought to understand more directly the world our students experienced, reflecting back to the student voices Noguera and his colleagues (2007) had so effectively captured. What if I did not simply interview, but rather invited students to join the inquiry with me? What might we learn if we together set out to understand the overlapping spaces of our distinct languages and cultures within the public space of schooling? Would they join an inquiry with this veteran white principal?

From among the former participants of the Dos Voces Program, I invited seven students—representative broadly of the demographics of the program. The group consisted of two students from English-speaking homes (Ashley and Brittany*), three students from bilingual homes (Bryan, Oscar, and Victoria), and two Spanish-speaking students (Ana and Camila). They agreed to meet in a group for discussions and individually for one-on-one conversations. We delved into their linguistic, cultural, and civic experiences over the years, raising new questions and insights for our work together in this community. The dynamics of our discussions were influenced by the closeness resulting from the students' long history together and my role as their principal beginning in kindergarten, staying in touch with them and their families over time. Still, our conversations were relatively stiff and superficial during the first focus group and our creation of a group identity map. In time, however, these discussions over pizza in the high school library as well as in my elementary school cafeteria evolved and became even deeper both during and after personal interviews.

Ultimately, our conversations unraveled all sorts of presumptions in our work and in my understanding of what was actually happening in the lives of our students in what I revered as our model program. For example, for all our championing of the virtues of bilingualism, these graduates of our dual language program rarely brought it up. When students created a collective identity map to represent their shared program experience, they rarely discussed bilingualism explicitly. I was also surprised that the students' dialogue during the week-long process of creating the map took place in English only, with Ana and Camila speaking minimal Spanish off to the side or when speaking to their parents on the phone.

Student interviews and focus groups uncovered how the separation of instruction into distinct English and Spanish zones may have influenced student perception of the purpose and appropriate setting for each language. Students shared that they spoke Spanish in the Spanish zone in elementary school, in Spanish classes in high school, and when speaking to a parent or peer who did not speak English. From these discussions, I reflected that the structural division of languages inherent in the design of our TWI program may have unintentionally reinforced the subordination of Spanish. From my observations and the students' analysis, English was and continues to be the dominant language.

INQUIRY INTO PRINCIPLES

García and colleagues (2011) use the concept of "third space" to analyze the ways that students of diverse language backgrounds communicate with each other. This

*Pseudonyms are used to protect the confidentiality of the students.

third space creates the setting for bicultural development and understanding, but could we see this "third space" among our students? Did it in fact exist, or were there English common spaces and, for Spanish side chats, only hallways? If I understood this "third space" more clearly, might we redesign our work toward a more robust bilingualism? How could we challenge the philosophical framework of TWI programs, a monoglossic perspective that accepts monolingualism as the norm and views bilingualism as double monolingualism?

In schools, we tend to identify students as English proficient and/or Spanish proficient. Among themselves, they understand a much more nuanced schema of language. In fact, each of the students described distinct socio-linguistic identities influenced by their families' different language use and their experiences. Could assignment of students by language proficiency undermine the goal of our work by categorizing students in simplistic ways that are also distant from their realities? As a leader, should I consider a more sophisticated classification of students' language designation upon entry to the program? Would this further open the learning spaces for students who come from homes composed of more than one language and culture?

UNDERSTANDING "THIRD SPACE": BENEFITS AND CHALLENGES

Despite limiting labels and clear English dominance, the students felt the program not only supported their cross-cultural (transcultural) understanding but helped Latino students embrace their heritage and cultural identity. For example, Ana and Camila, the most recent to arrive, both stated that they felt participation in the dual language program facilitated their transition to the United States, to school in America, and to speaking English. For the U.S. natives, Ashley and Brittany, White and Black respectively, the diversity of peers in the program provided them with insight into social issues (including immigration and the DREAM Act) that they felt their friends outside of Dos Voces lacked.

While much of the attention on the cultural benefits of TWI programs in the literature speaks to the impact of dual language programs on immigrants and U.S. native born children, a significant theme in the inquiry was the benefit for students from families of more than one cultural background to embrace the entirety of their heritage. Indeed, the most pronounced experiences of cultural benefits were shared by bilingual students. Oscar described how participation in Dos Voces helped him "integrate all aspects of himself," while Victoria said the experience made her "feel whole."

These cultural benefits appear to co-exist with a strengthening of what Nussbaum (1997) describes as circles of membership, or expanding layers of home and civic engagement. Specifically, students described being active in serving their families, participating meaningfully in the overall school program, and feeling a special sense of membership in the tight-knit Dos Voces program and community. Conversations with my student partners suggest that TWI programs that are designed to affirm linguistic and cultural diversity may have even greater potential to optimize civic identities and civic engagement. Interestingly, all students spoke of using their language skills to serve, the ultimate act of civic engagement. For example, Ashley translated for Spanish-speaking students and helped children at her dance studio; Bryan translated and read from the Bible in Spanish at church; Brittany and Oscar used their bilingual skills to read to students and help translate for families at the public library; Victoria volunteered at Summer School and translated for the students' parents; while Ana and Camila translated for their own families and for families attending the elementary school's Back-to-School nights. As a leader, I wonder how we might intentionally incorporate the cross-cultural use of language to fulfill service requirements, calling out publicly the benefits of bilingual/bicultural skills. Might we suggest that our students, beyond national boundaries even, coordinate virtual collaboration with students from schools in other countries, to use language skills authentically while working together to solve international problems?

Indeed, the program had brought students together from various parts of the world. My student inquiry partners spoke of the centrality of the close relationships they developed over the 10 years they learned together. Student interactions, however, revealed that this served to both include and exclude. While students mostly described using their language skills to serve and make others comfortable, they also described how they would sometimes switch languages to keep their conversations private. Mostly, however, student discussions revealed how their bond created during 10 years of learning together bilingually enabled them to sustain their transcultural relationships in the high school setting where most other students socialized in homogenous cultural groups (i.e., "most of the White kids hang out with other White kids, Spanish kids hang out with Spanish kids from their own [native] country, and the Black kids hang out with other Black kids" (personal communication, July 15, 2014).

Navigating cultural awareness is heavy terrain for all of us, and students would benefit from assistance in this journey. If it is not carefully designed, my students revealed, the exploration of culture is left to individual teachers and may not develop cohesively over the school experience. For example, students reported that they learned extensively about Uruguay because they had several teachers from that country, but did not learn formally about many other Latin American countries or cultures. TWI educators have an opportunity to create conditions where students uncover a deeper sense of cross-cultural understanding than celebration of festivals, food, and native dress can deliver. It became clear that in the effort to open up curricula, we can also inadvertently close out those whose prior dominance we may have been countering. For example, Ashley and Brittany described what they perceived as an overemphasis on Latino culture. While we felt that had been necessary during the design phase to resist the prevalence of native-born U.S. culture, Brittany's experience of not seeing herself represented in the cultural celebrations of the program raised a significant issue for us. Brittany revealed that she did not know "who to root for" or what to wear during heritage celebrations.

This revelation underscores the vacuum of opportunity that Brittany and probably other Black and culturally diverse students in the program have had to explore and embrace their respective heritages. It also points to TWI educators' need to thoughtfully support Black students' development while simultaneously resisting the subordination of the Spanish language and Latino cultures. Interestingly, Ashley described a similar experience of not knowing how to represent her culture because she did not have a particular connection to any of the several European heritages of her ancestors. How do I, as a leader, create space for cultural exchange, and include students whose cultural roots may feel tenuous or unclear?

POWER AND PRIVILEGE

As we continued our inquiry together, we dug further into issues of power, class, and race with each other. This discussion is best contextualized by the various perspectives students brought to the conversation. Ashley's previously mentioned perspective of not having a particular ethnic connection is an important distinction of her experience in the world that differs from the other students. DiAngelo (2012) describes the lack of connection to culture as a phenomenon of whiteness, where Whites do not see their color because it is the norm—often leading to the perception of culture and color as belonging only to "the other," namely non-Whites. Whiteness grants material and psychological advantages (i.e., White privilege) that are often invisible and taken for granted by Whites. While these factors are identified as the socialization of whiteness, Ashley (and other White students in TWI programs) do not necessarily experience all aspects of White socialization due to conversations with diverse peers.

For example, White students in TWI programs do not experience the same level of rewards for racial silence via White solidarity as they would in monolingual and monocultural settings. According to Sleeter (1996), White solidarity refers to the unspoken agreement among Whites not to talk openly and honestly about race and to avoid causing another White person to feel racial discomfort by confronting them when they say or do something racially problematic. Participation in TWI programs may also interrupt the socialization of what DiAngelo terms as "allowed racial innocence," which forgives ignorance as naivety (DiAngelo, p. 154). Many White students may have no sense of loss in racial segregation; DiAngelo identifies this as the final condition of White racial socialization. Yet Ashley (and I hope other White students in TWI programs) describe investment in their cross-cultural environment and friendships. While Ashley and other White TWI students are bound to experience dissonance in the complexity of these dynamics—for example, her mother and friends outside of dual language often saw such programs as unfair to White students—she still holds a position of privilege within the group. Interestingly, while she spoke the greatest number of times, her views often did not represent the majority in the context of the group or in the wider program.

Beyond whiteness, our inquiry revealed length of time in the United States as another power hierarchy. Camila was disappointed that she was omitted from the collective identity map owing to her more recent arrival. Both girls who immigrated to the country during the program spoke significantly less than other students, and were noticeably quiet during all conversations about race and privilege. Poignantly, they were completely silent during conversations about immigration and the DREAM Act.

Regardless of the time students spent in the program, their lives intersected in the third space it opened, where they learned, often informally, about one another's cultures and language. Of course, we found that this third space is not a neutral playing field, and students noted that, unguarded, it could replicate wider societal trends rather than transform them, particularly in light of anti-immigrant rhetoric to which our students are exposed. Lack of citizenship status was the glaring contrast to privilege as identified in student conversations.

Velasquez (2013) paints a personal picture of current immigration, resonant in the Ossining context, asserting that immigrants are here in part due to the pull of being employed as their neighbors' landscapers, house cleaners, and nannies. For fear of deportation, they are unlikely to report crimes against them or to seek medical care or assistance from any uniformed service that would draw attention to them. Velasquez comments that many immigrants from South American countries have embarked on journeys that very few of us can relate to: trying to cross the border to attain the American Dream of life, liberty, and the pursuit of happiness. Sadly and strikingly, Velasquez's description of adult immigrants as invisible and voiceless extends to their children, who are less vocal and less visible than their American-born peers, as our inquiry made evident. We learned, though, that we can structure the space for more of those voices to be heard, and to be understood in their agency.

LEADING AND LEARNING FROM INQUIRY

I began wrestling with how we might share school spaces across our cultures in Ossining back in 1995, when we began as a community to welcome yet another new set of immigrant cultures. In this most recent inquiry with my student partners, I learned that a cross-linguistic, cross-cultural environment increases the power of their voices, makes them more empathetic to a wider range of students, and enables them to be more active and engaged citizens with a broader representation of their community. It was also apparent from critical analysis of the interactions in the inquiry that TWI programs can be socially reproductive rather than socially transformative. In other words, TWI programs represent a concentrated microcosm of the community, and if greater value is given to English (majority) language and American (majority) culture and greater reinforcement is given to English speakers' Spanish skills, the program serves to exaggerate rather than resist the marginalization of the language minority students they are designed to serve. Accordingly, as leaders we must create structures and activities that consciously validate the Spanish language and respective cultures.

Our students powerfully shared how immigrant students use their robust bilingualism to manifest a transcultural civic identity and serve their communities. Students used their linguistic abilities to translate for their families and other students, in the public library, in church, and in the community at large. In this complex time, the facilitation of transculturalism—the ability to see the humanity in others who are different as well as those who are similar—is more necessary than ever. The development of effective TWI programs will be vital as increasing numbers of Latino immigrants move to suburban and rural districts.

One of my student partners stated eloquently her take on the experience of speaking two languages in the Dos Voces Un Mundo Program. Brittany noted:

> There is only a thin line between cultures. I thought this thin line would have been much thicker between cultures and groups. Being in Ossining (and not participating in dual language), I would have had some Spanish friends, but being in dual language, I have almost all Spanish friends . . . Language thins the line. I think I am more culturally accepting because of it. (Dealy, 2015, p. 69)

Our students invite us to optimize the potential of third spaces where students develop transcultural competencies. They urge us, as adults leading in their community, to thin these lines ourselves.

As a veteran school leader and practitioner researcher, one formidable learning challenge for me concerned where "the data" would come from. I was so locked into prescribed modes of collecting evidence or of coming in externally to "sample" student views that I originally presumed my creative collective identity map exercise, interview questions, and focus group protocols would provide the most information. These proved useful, but painfully static. I ultimately realized that the rounds of discussions and insights from and with these amazing young adults challenged presumptions and interrogated the evidence in ways impossible to consider from my positionality. Observations and reflections throughout our time together yielded equally important information, providing a window into the group dynamics and communication. I also viewed responses to questions about bilingualism; bicultural, transcultural and civic identity development; civic engagement; and social justice to be connected but separate responses. Corresponding discussions and observations helped me to see how deeply interconnected they are as a group. As our work evolved, the students and I realized that while they did not use the terms bicultural/transcultural, civic identity, civic engagement, or social justice until they were formally introduced in the focus group, all of these concepts were present before in the insights they shared. As a result, my commitment to practitioner inquiry as well as the values of bilingualism, transculturalism, and civic engagement is more deeply etched upon my heart and mind.

Nonetheless, I have also learned that deep dedication to a vision of excellence and equity; the cultivation of bilingualism, biliteracy, and biculturalism; and the implementation of best-researched models of equitable practice is a start—but it is not enough. My leadership learnings include the necessity for collective inquiry to affect systemic change. My ongoing inquiry has shifted my view of the experience we hope for all students; our prior vision does not match their reality. In order for us to bridge to a new vision, it will require ongoing reflection and response of every member of our District community. Fortunately, I see evidence that our long effort to make meaning of our multiple cultural contexts continues to deepen. Under the leadership of our current superintendent, Ray Sanchez, we have again taken on equity work with the NYU Metro Center and specifically Director Natalie McCabe Zwerger. Through our newly formed District Equity Committee—comprised of parents, community members, educators, and most importantly students—we are committed to creating structures and systems that lift student voices so as to realize lasting change. These efforts include equitable communication methods; ongoing study, implementation, and review of representative and responsive curriculum; and identification of disparities through regular study of disaggregated academic, behavioral, and attendance data. Embedding more locally, school-level equity committees have been formed and will now lead local professional development on racial literacy and overall climate consciousness from an equity lens.

Our collective inquiry, if a slow evolution, now brings me renewed faith as this more systemic approach and shared commitment seeks to bring us closer to delivering on the mission of our District to our richly diverse Hudson Valley community.

REFERENCES

Costello, A. (1994, March 6). 20 years after Ossining's riots, mood of racial harmony prevails. *New York Times*. Retrieved from www.nytimes.com/1994/03/06/nyregion/20-years-after-ossining-s-riots-mood-of-racial-harmony-prevails.html?pagewanted=all

Dealy, A. E. (2015). *"Language thins the line": The cultural development of dual language graduates: A reciprocal relationship between language, culture, and civic identity development* (Doctoral dissertation). Retrieved from ProQuest Dissertations & Theses Database. (UMI No. 3746325).

DiAngelo, R. J. (2012). *What does it mean to be White?: Developing white racial literacy.* New York, NY: Peter Lang.

Flemming, A. S., Horn, C. S., Freeman, F. M., Ruiz, M., Jr., & Saltzman, M. (1977). *Reviewing a decade of school desegregation, 1966–1975.* Washington, DC: U.S. Commission on Civil Rights.

García, O., Makar, C., Starcevic, M., & Terry, A. (2011). The translanguaging of Latino kindergarterners. In K. Potowski & J. Rothman (Eds.), *Bilingual youth: Spanish in English-speaking societies* (pp. 33–55). Amsterdam, Netherlands: John Benjamins Publishing.

McKinney, M. P., & Fitz-Gibbon, J. (June 9, 2017). ICE agents arrest high schooler hours before prom. *USA Today*. Retrieved from www.usatoday.com/story/news/nation-now/2017/06/09/high-school-student-immigration-arrest/385457001/

Noguera, P., Sealey-Ruiz, Y., Fergus, E., Christodoulou, M., Handville, N., Meade, B., & Torres, M. (2007). *Charting the course of excellence for all: The Ossining High School Diversity Project (Rep.)*. New York, NY: The Metropolitan Center for Urban Education.

Nussbaum, M. (1997). Kant and stoic cosmopolitanism. *The Journal of Political Philosophy*, 5, 1–25.

Sleeter, C. E. (1996). White silence, White solidarity. In N. Ignatiev & J. Garvey (Eds.), *Race traitors* (pp. 257–265). New York, NY: Routledge.

Velasquez, J. C. (2013). The invisible & voiceless: The plight of the undocumented immigrant in America. Available at business-ethics.com/2014/09/30/1944-the-invisible-voiceless-the-plight-of-the-undocumented-immigrant-in-america/

CHAPTER 3

Learning to Lead from the Middle

Students' Feedback on Feedback

Martha A. Richmond

Martha A. Richmond is the coordinator of academic advising and educational support and the assistant director of multicultural affairs for academics at the Seconsett School,* a 200-year old institution enrolling students from 36 countries and 38 states. She draws upon her work in inclusion, equity, and culturally responsive pedagogy in both roles, and while they initially appear separate, Richmond believes they share a common goal of helping all students feel they justly belong to the school community. She earned an EdD in educational leadership from the University of Pennsylvania as well as master's degrees in education from Teachers College, Columbia University, and Boston University, where she also earned a BS in broadcasting and film. Marti earned her school psychology certificate at Rider University.

Every day in schools, students experience messages of belonging and social connectedness. Students at my school, and in most other schools, receive feedback in an array of modes and means. In addition to face-to-face interactions, feedback also comes in the form of teachers' handwritten comments on essay papers, as inserted comments on an electronic assignment, or in the more summative form of a handwritten or an electronic report card. Messages may be explicitly expressed through feedback, or more implicitly couched in school traditions that also send signals to students about who they are, how they are regarded by teachers, and how well they are responding to expectations and challenges.

As a school psychologist and the coordinator of educational support in a highly selective and competitive school, I have often wondered about the power of these messages, especially with regard to our most academically vulnerable students. Feedback is not just a cognitive process but an emotional and cultural experience as well, and it has great sway on how students thrive and the self-narratives they construct about their ability to learn, meet challenges, and belong.

In our school, another established way students receive feedback is via our electronic memo system. These memos, now delivered by email, allow our teachers

*The name of the school is a pseudonym, used to protect confidentiality.

to communicate with their students and their advisors and with their students' parents on a regular basis outside of formal reporting periods. While now an electronic mode of feedback, according to our library archivist, as a feedback practice the memo system possesses a 125-year history in our school. This long tradition speaks to the wide, but untested, academic agreement on the importance of our memo system for student learning at my school.

Recognizing that this feedback custom has carried on in various formats for over a century, I found myself inquiring about what makes feedback effective (or ineffective) in general. In addition, with respect to my school and my responsibilities, I questioned how both colleagues and students regard the effectiveness of our memo system. My inquiry into this institution became a two-part story. First, it was an exploration of what I could learn from listening closely to some of my school's most academically vulnerable students about the ways they receive and understand feedback. Although our memo system is unique to our school, I think the students' stories and the relational lens that they used to talk about their teachers and feedback suggests a more universal narrative about this potentially emancipatory piece of pedagogy (see Richmond, 2011). (Yorke [2003] notes that formative feedback "[encourages] emancipation by alerting the student to possibilities which he had not hitherto discerned" [p. 478].) The second part of this story explores how the practice of inquiry emancipated my own sense of efficacy as I realized that inquiry empowered me with the means to test and reframe unchallenged school narratives about our memo system as well as to unpack my own narratives about what it means to lead from the middle.

COLLEAGUES TEACH ME ABOUT FEEDBACK AND LEADERSHIP

In my role as Coordinator of Academic Advising and Educational Support, I work under our academic dean assisting students struggling academically. I do so by working directly with students and colleagues and by coordinating other offerings such as workshops and supervising our department's part-time learning specialists. I also think a lot about practice as it pertains to students under academic pressure. The fact that I ended up in this role as an advocate for the academically vulnerable (and that I attained a graduate school degree) is both surprising and not surprising. I had struggled through school as a student with an undiagnosed learning disability, and in high school, my parents were advised by my guidance counselor that maybe I was not 4-year college material. Additionally, I am now also the parent of a daughter with special needs. So, I know first-hand that grit and resilience without effective strategies and feedback are not sustainable. Given the importance of feedback, I began to wonder about our school's student feedback system called academic memos. These memos are electronic email-like missives that faculty can send at will to their students as a supplement to traditional modes of feedback written on papers and other assessments.

According to our faculty handbook:

> Academic memos allow faculty to communicate with students, advisors, and parents on a regular basis, outside of the final reporting periods. Academic memos can be labeled "commendation," "concern," and "possible failure." . . . "Internal" memos are sent to the [student] and the student's advisor; "external" memos are sent to parents as well.

I knew most of our school's discussion on feedback focused on whether it was formative or summative, but I was interested in the patterns of our memo system rather than the individual actions of faculty and students. My preliminary research into the memos had shown the feedback to be mostly summative, such as reporting a grade or simply beckoning the student to see the teacher. With the help of our school archivist, I learned that these academic memos began as a school practice in the 1800s.

Tradition is important in my school, but given current understandings about learning, I believed this feedback practice could be missing its mark for offering students formative feedback and for looking at patterns of practice my dean could use for planning professional development. I was curious to learn if the memos sent by my colleagues established any patterns during the school year, such as systemic patterns of student or teacher difficulties or patterns related to the social identities of our teachers or students. How did students receive the feedback messaged in these electronic missives? Could the answers to these questions point to actionable interventions that would lead to value-added student learning? My questions were rooted in my abiding commitment to more equitable outcomes for students whose performance indicated that as a school we had not yet met their academic needs. As far as I knew, no one had ever looked at the effects of these 200-year-old academic missives.

I reached out to six colleagues with whom I had already been meeting weekly. Our group had grown out of a mutual interest in making our school a place where all students felt a sense of belonging. While we shared this commitment, we had not come up with an actual inquiry plan, so I proposed we look at the memos faculty sent to struggling students. In pairs, wondering what race- and gender-based patterns might emerge, we decided to categorize 78 randomly picked memos sent to juniors whose grades did not reflect their predicted potential.

Our investigation generated two broad categories (positive and negative memos) that could be refined with nuanced subcategories. Through our discussions, I found some of my early assumptions both challenged and refined. I had regarded memos containing only a teacher's invitation to come for consultation as negative, but the others saw these overtures as nurturing outreach. The group opened me to new interpretations, an important stance if I wanted to genuinely inquire into our practice and lead colleagues in questioning entrenched habits of practice.

STUDENTS TEACH ME ABOUT FEEDBACK AND ABOUT LEADERSHIP

If listening to my colleagues broadened my understanding of our memo system and of ways I could lead conversations about school traditions, then what would I learn from listening to the students? I had thought about how my having been a student who struggled shaped my views about memos, but since my inquiry involved students of color, I now wondered how my identity as a White faculty member would affect their willingness to share their experiences and my ability to interpret their responses. Even as I had worked hard to be an ally to my colleagues of color, I knew from my own student experiences that it is a difficult experience to expose feelings of vulnerability and marginalization as a student. So I asked a Black colleague in our group, Lucinda,** to help. Together, we invited students to join one of two focus groups.

From our group's initial work, I refined the questions I had originally considered. Now, I wondered:

- How do our students who struggle academically perceive and experience academic memos?
- How do these students make meaning of the feedback in these memos?
- What do these students see as the benefits and drawbacks of the system?
- How do students' gender, race, and ethnicity mediate this process?

After the focus groups, Lucinda and I looked for themes that could be pursued in individual conversations with students. Given our different backgrounds, Lucinda raised distinctions I had missed. While I noted racial differences in the types of memos students discussed, Lucinda highlighted class differences among the Black students as well as racial differences in the amount of deference students extended to their teachers and the messages in the memos. The recursive work of reviewing these together helped me see more distilled insights.

As Lucinda and I continued to discuss emerging themes, I kept a diary that helped clarify my biases and served as sounding board for emerging questions. If writing helped me refine my internal dialogues, working closely with a colleague of color helped me refine ways to talk about race and to enter the difficult conversations often silenced in our diverse but polite academic community. Lucinda's insights about race, and her feedback, helped me grow as an inquirer and as a person.

In addition to raising my racial consciousness, the conversations with Lucinda also raised additional questions I wanted to use as follow-up with students. Each of these one-on-one conversations took approximately 45 minutes as I asked the students to elaborate on comments made in their focus group. By reflecting back focus group observations to the students in our one-on-one meetings, I could verify information from the focus groups. Wanting to know more about their individual experiences, I printed out their previous term memos and asked each student to

**A pseudonym is used to protect confidentiality.

rate two of his or her personal memos. By doing so, I could compare their reactions with those of the rating committee.

Although Lucinda did not interview the students, she transcribed three of the conversations and wrote summaries of main ideas. We compared students' responses, and I found myself wondering about the degree to which race and gender were part of the relational context of the memo system. While I recognized that the authority of my inquiry would be created through the voices of the students and my colleagues, reading Miriam Raider-Roth's work (2005) has helped frame my lens as an educator. I recollected her description of the relational contexts in which learning occurs in school, and how "students come to know their teachers and peers and discern what interactions will sustain these social connections and which will undermine them" (p. 587). I realized that using this relational lens offered a novel and important way to understand students' receptivity to their memos. Indeed, as Lucinda and I listened to the students, we realized that these relationships were complicated by race, class, gender, and the preexisting relationships students had with their classroom teachers from outside activities such as athletics, clubs, and school trips.

Pulling together the ranking of the memos, the summaries of the focus groups, and the individual student conversations, I looked for patterns as well as responses that would enrich my understanding of student reactions to their academic memos. While my overriding interest remained feedback, I found reading about race and the relational context of learning helped me to observe common themes in the reactions. The student voices and Lucinda's observations told a story about feedback that had not been heard before. To look for patterns, I designed a chart that categorized responses by student gender and race. For example, in the focus groups and in interviews, most Black students described receiving negative memos and their experiences were borne out with the memo rating chart.

Patterns were identified in three major areas: (1) gender and racial patterns, (2) the relational context of feedback, and (3) suggestions for making memos more formative. The relational context included the different effects created by positive and negative memos, uncertainty over the true intended audience of memos, and the relationships of students with adults (parents, teachers, and advisors) when they had received negative memos.

The salience of student–teacher relationships struck me. Students felt teacher care when they read formative memos, and admitted feeling embarrassed that they had let down their teacher after receiving a memo indicating they had performed poorly on an assessment or assignment. As students reflected on "bad" and "good" memos, I wondered how these memos affected the ways students who struggle academically constructed narratives about who they were as learners and about their belongingness in our school community. Because I found no literature on the importance of the relational context of feedback, I wondered how I could help students share that they read their memos through a lens of relationships with their teachers. Before listening to these students, I had not given thought to how the students had "read" my own memos or how my feedback and students' reactions got woven into their sense of efficacy and identity.

INQUIRING INTO PATTERNS OF TEACHER FEEDBACK

Beyond student reactions to the memos, I wondered what information my dean would find helpful for planning professional development. Overall, I discovered my findings could be grouped into three areas. First, I noted both gender- and race-related patterns. For example, boys received more memos than girls. This pattern reflected an earlier outside audit of our school that had found that the school still places boys at the center of school. I found myself wondering if the school's 175-year history of being an all-boys school and its merely 25-year history of coeducation were playing out in our feedback system. So much of the school's material makeup reflected gender inequity: the quality of our dormitories; our interscholastic offerings; the unequal ratio of male to female students on campus and in student government. I wondered if it could be that in the school's other practices, such as teacher feedback, gender inequality was also manifest.

My wonderings gained substance when I read further in the audit that a significant number of faculty confessed that because they believed girls were more emotional than boys, they were less inclined to give them feedback. During her interview one girl said, "I actually would like to get more [memos]. It would be nice since then you know the teacher has noticed you." I wondered about the consequences of a student's missing a viable form of transmitting feedback, especially if it were a girl needing to learn how to negotiate a school that appeared to still function as a traditionally male institution. In addition, such student feedback suggested that faculty beliefs about girl's' receptivity needed a forum for exploration.

In addition, my chart suggested race-related patterns to the sending of memos. Black students received fewer memos overall than White students, and Black students were less likely than White students to receive positive memos. For example, one Black male student, thinking his experience reflected an overall pattern, observed, "I feel that most memos are negative. There are a few positive ones, but most tend to be negative." I began to wonder: Were my colleagues aware that our historically marginalized students, girls and Black students, received fewer memos than boys and White students? And if students saw feedback as a form of connection and care, how did this relative lack of feedback affect their sense of belonging?

During one focus group, another Black male noted: "Yeah, but I got some good ones, but like say, if I get an A on something I won't get a memo for that, but, say, if I happen to fail something like that then I get a memo." Not only did Black students in my survey receive more negative memos, they received so few positive memos that they experienced that type of feedback as an anomaly.

Negative memos were not just the experience of the Black male students. A Black female shared her experience with negative memos:

> It happened to me last spring one teacher consistently sent me bad memos really every single day and eventually my mum had to call her and tell her that X doesn't respond well to this type of negative feedback and if you are trying to get her to do better don't just criticize her on a daily basis.

During her interview this Black female continued: "Eventually I felt like I could never do anything right in class." Given that a Seconsett School precept is that improved performance and learning requires directed and ongoing feedback from faculty, this finding suggested that girls and Black students find themselves at an academic disadvantage.

As these findings took form, Lisa Delpit's (2006) assertion, "that success in institutions—schools, workplaces, and so on—is predicated upon acquisition of the culture of those who are in power" (p. 25) bore into me. I wondered what effect these memos or lack of memos had on the self-narratives of some of our most academically vulnerable students.

MY LEARNING FROM THE STUDENTS' FEEDBACK ON FEEDBACK

In addition to recognizing that gender and race were part of my school's memo story, I heard other themes, including students' desire for dialogue with teachers in the face of negative feedback and their discomfort re-entering the classroom after receiving a negative memo. Although most students voiced a need for memos, they felt the school's current system needed revision, and their responses reflected the importance of relationships when receiving feedback from teachers. Additionally, the students' responses reflected different levels of deference to their teachers, revealing contrasting feelings of privilege by White and Black students.

As students referred to the way memos made them think about their connections with their teachers, I noticed that this theme of social connection manifested in several ways. For example, their responses shared an awareness of the power faculty held over them. One student critiqued, "They [the memos] are kinda like a big power trip for them [the teachers]." Particularly for memos with a negative message, the students yearned for face-to-face interactions with their teachers. As one student surmised:

> It's almost like they are shy—you are a teacher and the memo—like a lover—this is how I really feel about you [sic]. I understand it . . . is hard to pull a kid aside but . . . SAY SOMETHING. I mean just don't let it slide and act as if everything is normal.

Listening to the students, it became clear to me that while the students craved more direct contact with teachers regarding negative memos, they reveled when they received positive feedback via memos. As one girl acknowledged, "It's a nice boost of self-confidence when she says like I have had improvement and she is kinda noticing that. She is not just like noting the grades, she is noting improvement which is nice."

Although I heard the students expressing differing standards and responses to negative and positive memos, their responses to both revealed the implicit power relationship between faculty and students. Most poignantly, they described feeling it keenly when they return to class the day after receiving what they construed as a "bad" memo. Listening to the students, I realized that my colleagues needed to hear about the disconnecting effect of negative memos. How could they mend the fabric of a relationship when there was no policy in place to facilitate the follow-up needed? If these "bad" memos led to a sense of disconnection between students and teachers and, more importantly, to a sense of disconnection between students and their ability to learn, how pedagogically effective could they be? What role did the resulting sense of disconnection play for our most vulnerable students? As one Black girl noted, "The worst is when you get a really bad memo and the next day you have to go to class and sit there with that teacher." To which another concurred, "The teacher has no clue of the aftermath of [the] memo." Similarly, in an interview, another Black student, a male, remembered, "So, the next day in the class I am waiting, you venting on me in the memo and you never talk about it at all and go on to the class."

Student emphasis on their desire for direct feedback from their teachers in lieu of negative feedback sent via memos appeared especially moving for the Black students. They were less likely than White students to receive positive memos, and they expressed more deference to their teachers and to the content of their memos. In contrast, as the White students spoke, they were more likely to convey irreverence toward negative memos, such as:

> If you get a dumb one like a memo sent home to my parents saying I didn't do my homework, then I am just going to be mad at the teacher, and I am going into the classroom and pretend I didn't do my homework at first.

Likewise, another White male reported in his interview that "Sometimes they were really funny—if you got a bad memo, it was so ridiculous of what went wrong."

While White students used words such as ridiculous, funny, and dumb, I heard Black students express deference to their teachers and their feedback. Despite their disproportional share of negative memos, the Black students offered comments such as "The more severe ones are the ones that make me want to be better," and "When I get chewed out by the science teacher, I think yeah, that is exactly what I do, and I kinda' want to fix that." Just as the word "ridiculous" appeared a common theme for the White students, the word "fix" resonated with the Black students, as another Black student reacted to one of his many negative memos, "Listen, I have to fix it." Similarly, in her interview, one of the Black females said, "I challenge myself more to kinda prove the teacher wrong whatever I need to."

As I noticed these different reactions, I found myself wanting to share these responses with my dean as well as with my colleagues. I also wanted to share the finding that students value and need strategic feedback. In this regard, the students gave voice to and confirmed a bias that had initially informed my inquiry. Again, I found myself drawn to Miriam Raider-Roth (2005) and her assertion:

> it is not sufficient for teachers just to care. Teachers have to care enough, and the criteria of "enough" are measured by their actions of connection and response. The quality of response is vital because it is in this dialogue that his faith in what he knows about himself as a learner is constructed. (p. 593)

Thus, a comment from one student, "I never got a memo in class that really explained to me how I was doing," suggested that students feel let down in the quality of connection and response conveyed by faculty in the memos. Another student further illustrated this opinion, "I would really prefer a memo that says I got a 5 out of 50 on the quiz and here is what I should do. Like don't just tell me I got a 5 out of 50—like I already know." Similarly, another student elaborated:

> If you are sent out a concern memo, you list the concerns, if the teacher lists concerns with the student make sure to let the student have an idea of what they should do about it like coming into consultation to see the teacher or do more of their homework. Don't just point out why the student is struggling or having difficulty in class and give absolutely no solution and expect the student to change when they might be underperforming.

In contrast only one student seized upon her experience to describe a helpful memo, "So it is direction of what I should do because I did not do so well on the first test. It was helpful."

By listening to these students and to Lucinda, I learned that students crave feedback and connection to their teachers and that it is through these connections that the students form and construct narratives about their ability to learn or construct knowledge. But I also realized the fragility of these connections based on patterns of gender and race as well as by my colleagues' habit of sending summative rather than formative memos.

LISTENING AS LEADERSHIP

Beyond traditional ways of investigating feedback, my inquiry pointed to the deeply relational context of feedback including how feedback affected the self-narratives of our academically vulnerable students. I realized that my dean and my colleagues could develop a more informed understanding of our school's almost 200-year-old memo system if they heard our students' reactions to their memos. So I approached my dean, convinced that faculty needed a chance to hear these student voices and see the connection between relationships and feedback, and to hear how negative memos affected the self-narratives of our academically vulnerable students and their sense of academic efficacy. As I pondered my findings, a question that Miriam Raider-Roth (2005) asks haunted me: "How do the relationships of school life shape students' capacity to trust what they know?" (p. 587)

What My Colleagues Learned from My Inquiry

As a result of our meeting, my dean allocated time during the opening of school professional development to discuss our memo system. I was given a 2-hour session to meet with the faculty and asked each colleague to bring two memos they had written during the past year. During the session, I asked each colleague to do reflective writing that considered the purpose of their memo and how they thought the student reacted to it. When they finished their reflective writing, I presented the findings regarding the number of memos sent to students broken down by race and gender. After asking the colleagues to break into small groups, I distributed handouts that shared the voices of the students through their direct quotations, identified by their race and their gender. In their groups, I asked my colleagues to comb through the quotations to uncover themes. I reminded them to keep their conversations centered on the student voices.

It was the first time student voices were included in faculty professional development. Situating these conversations around student voice seemed important since "authorizing student perspectives introduces into critical conversations the missing perspectives of those who experience daily the effects of existing educational policies-in-practice" (Cook-Sather, 2002, p. 3). After the smaller groups reported back, I asked my colleagues to reread and revisit their earlier reflections. As they did, I passed out two sticky notes, and on one, I asked colleagues to write a personal take-away from the meeting that they could refer to when composing a memo. On their second sticky note, I asked them to write an institutional change they would recommend regarding the memo system. As a result of the workshops, faculty agreed to talk first with any student to whom they sent what students characterized as a "bad memo."

Moving Forward

In a conversation with my dean after our faculty workshop, we discarded what had been the school's practice of designating whether the memo was a concern or a commendation. Instead, we wrote an introductory statement to each memo:

> Dear ____________:
>
> Seconsett believes that students value and grow with feedback. This email serves to let you know that (teacher's name and subject) has written this comment for you to consider and discuss with your advisor.

To continue our discussion, during a regular monthly faculty meeting later in the term, we revisited the purpose and tone of memos. This time, the academic dean reminded the faculty of our earlier discussions on how we care for and give feedback to our students in order to promote learning. I framed our discussion along the paradigms of buttressing belonging, ethics of care, conveying a belief in student competence, and in terms of teacher presence. Since then, faculty discussion about feedback has continued. Our practice has become more dialogic. That is, teacher practices include talking to a student before sending a memo. Further, the head of our teaching and learning center held a summer forum on the importance of incorporating messages of challenge and belongingness into feedback. Additionally, student voices have become a mainstay in discussions that involve our school and in faculty meetings.

LEARNING ABOUT LEADERSHIP FROM AN INQUIRY STANCE

While this inquiry taught me about the relational context of feedback, it taught me even more about voice: that is, about the importance of listening to voices of experience—our own as practitioners as well as the voices of students—if we want to learn the effects of school traditions and practices. It taught me that the voices of personal experiences and our identities can sow the seeds of inquiry and that inquiry fosters the voices of practitioners, who do not lead from the top. I realized that although I am not a dean, by inquiring into stakeholders' experience I obtained tools and authority to make change in my school. On one level, the student voices from this inquiry altered the way I think about feedback. However, just as important, the inquiry altered the way I think about faculty, like me, who are not part of the senior staff but who, through taking an inquiry stance, have the ability to prompt change. I came to realize that through inquiry one can lead from the middle. From my experience with this inquiry, as I have come to profoundly appreciate the power of student voices in any discussion about practices that affect their lives, I have also come to profoundly appreciate the power inquiry gives to any faculty member wanting to improve their school and their practice.

REFERENCES

Cook-Sather, A. (2002). Authorizing students' perspectives: Toward trust, dialogue, and change in education. *Educational Researcher, 31*(4), 3–1.

Delpit, L. (2006). *Other people's children: Cultural conflict in the classroom*. New York, NY: The New Press.

Raider-Roth, M. B. (2005). Trusting what you know: Negotiating the relational context of classroom life. *Teachers College Record, 107*, 587–628.

Richmond, M. A. (2011). *Feedingback: Looking at an independent school's feedback system through a relational lens* (Doctoral dissertation). Retrieved from ProQuest Dissertations & Theses Database. (UMI No. 3455382).

Yorke, M. H. (2003). Formative assessment in higher education: Moves toward theory and the enhancement of pedagogic practice. *Education, 45*, 477–501.

CHAPTER 4

"Leaders Can Be Anyone"

Students and Teachers Sharing Inquiry

Peter Horn

Peter Horn became an independent education researcher, writer, and consultant after leading Project '79, the award-winning alternative education program within a suburban New Jersey high school. Horn has led research projects for Princeton University and the University of Pennsylvania, as well as professional development in public and independent schools and other organizations. He earned his doctorate from the University of Pennsylvania, an MA in English literature from the Middlebury Bread Loaf School of English, and a BA in Greek and Latin from Princeton University.

Inquiry can improve any kind of organization, but with students who find themselves at the margins of school, the stakes are particularly high. Providing opportunities for students to ask and answer questions about how school could be better is especially valuable for students (sometimes deemed "at risk") who have difficulty connecting with school as it is normally done. A teacher leader for 2 decades, I am passionate about the relationship between student voice, school-based opportunities to engage citizenship, and a more democratic society. For 7 years, I was the teacher leader in charge of Project '79, an alternative program within a public high school in suburban New Jersey. As coordinator, I led colleagues and taught English to students who had chosen to join Project '79 because they were seeking a different school experience. Our students did not connect with traditional approaches to education, for a variety of reasons. Some were poor test-takers, some were bored by what they were asked to learn, some had personal or family issues; most held other priorities over schoolwork. As one graduate put it, "I always struggled with the monotony of school, the typical stand-in-front, 'Write this down!' 'Listen!' I'm open to new ways to try and learn things because the standard doesn't work with me. I just don't click with that."

My coordinator role also entailed leading a team of eight talented, hardworking colleagues teaching art, English, math, science, and social studies. Every day we sat at a round table for 40 minutes, discussing our students, meeting with them and their parents, trying to dream up new ways to engage our students as more self-directed learners. One week we brainstormed a collaboration between our chemistry and art teachers that challenged students to design and construct a massive installation in the stairwell of the science wing in order to demonstrate just how big a mole of sand (or 6.02×10^{23} units) would be. Another time, we schemed plans to program a mini-TEDx conference with our sophomores as expert presenters. The following story of shared inquiry grows out of meetings around that conference table where Project '79 teachers began to see an opportunity to engage our students differently as collaborators. Since the program's inception in 1979, Project '79 has been rooted in rigor, relevance, and teacher–student relationships. It has a strong tradition of listening to students in order to reconnect struggling learners to school, and teachers expect that students will take advantage of the supports Project '79 offers (such as individualized tutoring and after-school study halls) in order to learn more and better than they have in school before. In the words of a current student, Project '79 "provides a more individualized and personal way of education." Classes are designed to be as relevant as possible, clarifying the practical value of the work assigned and encouraging student input into units of study. For instance, seniors in my 2014–2015 English IV class chose to read Mohamedou Ould Slahi's just-published *Guantánamo Diary* as a nonfiction companion to our Kafka unit. Professional artists lead residencies that guide students to express their ideas and questions through public works of theater, poetry, and music. The staff artist-in-residence provides opportunities for students to express themselves through sculpture, painting, and film. Teacher–student relationships are enriched by smaller class sizes and daily staff meetings, but also by field trips and activities such as the 2-day retreat to the Princeton Blairstown Center each fall, which focuses on team-building, peer leadership, and communication skills. As another current student has noted, "Teachers and students alike learn from and teach each other. As a community, we come together to support each other and encourage each other."

CLASSROOM TECHNOLOGY AS ADAPTIVE CHALLENGE

For a number of years, our school district seemed to be flailing when it came to classroom technology. Faculty members discussed technology frequently, and the district made it the center of several professional development sessions. Laptop carts were rolled from classroom to classroom by teachers who spent the first and last minutes of each class unpacking and packing devices. Sporadic experimentation with varied learning activities occurred. There were some trailblazers in the high school, such as the American Studies class where students used iPads every day with explicit aims of better collaboration and more student ownership of learning. Most of us, however, without consistent access to tools or embedded professional development to prod and guide, were only tinkering at the edges of how we did school (e.g., PowerPoints instead of overhead projections).

Fortunately, this realization coincided with my graduate study in organizational leadership, which introduced me to the difference between *technical problems* and *adaptive challenges.* Heifetz and Linsky (2002) define *technical problems* as those that can be solved by people in charge who apply established knowledge to the trouble at hand. To many educators this was more or less the way our district seemed to be viewing instructional technology: various devices, apps, and platforms seemed to appear haphazardly, like buckshot bullet-points from somebody's 5-year plan.

The organizational leadership classes I was taking at about this time prompted me to reframe the perennial issue of technology. We as Project '79 staff could choose to frame it as an *adaptive challenge* rather than a *technical problem* and derive many opportunities to engage our students differently in what and how they learned. According to Heifetz and Linsky (2002), *adaptive challenges* require "experiments, new discoveries, and adjustments from numerous places in the organization or community" in order for people to thrive in a new environment (p. 13). In the context of the ongoing technological revolution that has spurred seismic shifts in what it means to be literate, how we communicate, and how businesses and markets operate (Davidson, 2011), Project '79 began to re-imagine an approach to classroom technology with a focus on opportunities for students to help us experiment, adjust, and make new discoveries. Our program was well positioned to innovate by our small footprint (eight teachers, 91 students) and collaborative structure.

Furthermore, I subscribed fully to the argument advanced by Cook-Sather (2002) that educators need to "authorize" student perspectives, because doing so "recognizes and responds to the profound and unprecedented ways in which the world has changed and continues to change, and the position students occupy in relation to this change" (p. 4). In other words, as a result of their immersion in technology, many students acquire informal expertise that could help schools do education better. "Authorization" is Cook-Sather's metaphor for educators' willingness to listen to students, take their ideas seriously, and allow opportunities for students and teachers to work together to co-construct educational experiences.

For some educators, however, the prospect of authorizing students in this way is intimidating. Part of my job in running daily meetings was to maintain a safe space to talk candidly about our work, including the fears that held us back. Some of us, for example, felt trepidation about understanding less than our students about certain aspects of technology, a threat to any teacher who sees their prime role as "knower." We discussed questions like: "If students suddenly have access to all the information on the Internet, not to mention all the stimulating modes in which that information is presented, what are teachers doing in the room?" Reframing our situation as an adaptive challenge let Project '79 staff pose a new question: "What if teachers tried to benefit from the ways that students are 'differently knowledgeable about a range of new modes of communication and uses for education' (Cook-Sather, 2002, p. 4) than we are?" Project '79 staff members agreed that students needed to have a seat at the table for our upcoming meeting.

The Project '79 Tech Vision Summit

On a spring afternoon in New Jersey, 13 adults and three students sat in a horseshoe in the Project '79 office, facing a problem on the whiteboard: *How can Project '79 best use technology for teaching and learning?* Three students were not a lot to represent our 91 student members, but three would have to do, because the guest list was already close to capacity for a beneficial 1-hour exchange of ideas. The 16 stakeholders included the Assistant Superintendent of Curriculum and Instruction, one Board of Education member, the K–12 Guidance Supervisor, the High School Master Technology Teacher, the Assistant Principal leading technology initiatives, our program's Parent Coordinator, a freelance tech consultant, five of our program teachers, and three students. My thought was that the diversity of roles would help us see different angles of the technology situation. The students were a freshman with a strong interest in fantasy fiction who described his parents as "neo-Luddites"; a sophomore who had decided in 8th grade that she wanted to become a forensic scientist; and a tech-savvy senior who generally favored the safety of strident cynicism, recently declaring in class, "Everything this school does with technology is totally backwards!" I didn't know how much our students would say in a conversation with so many unfamiliar adults, but I wanted them to have the experience of sitting at the table as equal participants. I planned to follow up with each of them afterward to compare notes.

At the start of the meeting, I invoked the potential of conversation among stakeholders with different perspectives on a given problem and asked the group not to worry yet about possible financial or legal constraints; these would be addressed *after* we developed goals for instructional technology to improve teaching and learning. My brief introduction concluded with the observation that we are trying to prepare students to participate in a rapidly-changing world in which some of them will hold jobs that do not even exist today. The discussion was fast-paced and wide-ranging. We surveyed digital learning throughout our building, including the American Studies course with daily access to iPads, where students reported that the tenor of the classroom was more dynamic because of their ability to research anything instantly and independently. Teachers laid out what we understood about learners: Many Project '79 students struggle with organization and asking for help, so how could personal devices aid in these areas? We considered logistics, such as the pros and cons of school-supplied vs. home-supplied devices, and what types of devices (laptop, tablet, phone). We discussed socioeconomic dimensions, such as equity of access to technology for all students. We also interrogated some philosophical tenets of Project '79, such as our aim for learning to be as authentic as possible, reducing the infamous rift between school and "the real world." Since so much of what we produce and consume relies on the Internet, shouldn't we acknowledge its education potential for all students? Finally, we discussed suggestions about which stakeholders to approach next, and how.

The Tech Vision Summit served several purposes. First, it let Project '79 staff check blind spots. I felt pretty good that we had already surfaced many of these issues during our meetings. Second, the gathering garnered greater buy-in from people outside the program who were now included in our conversation. As a step toward authorizing student voices in our deliberations, we had young people around the table listening attentively, often leaning forward and occasionally taking notes. They commented a few times and responded frankly when asked by another participant what they thought. When I met with them later, students provided insights and suggestions about, for example, the viability of one platform over another. They appreciated being asked to attend, with one praising the opportunity to share viewpoints in a non-condescending, respectful atmosphere. The meeting was a positive step toward student engagement, but it was not sufficient to change attitudes, values, and behaviors in the way Heifetz and Linsky (2002) argue an "adaptive leap" entails: "The sustainability of change depends on having the people with the problem internalize the change itself" (p. 13). What could an adaptive leap look like for Project '79, I wondered. Would it be possible for our teachers and students to internalize a different vision of not only technology in the classroom, but also student participation in co-designing the aims and activities of learning?

Determining the Work

Despite how important student perspectives would be to this process, I believed it was necessary for teachers to take the next step, goal-setting, during closed team meetings. This way, colleagues who were not as enthusiastic about pending shifts in classroom routines could have space without a student audience to air their concerns. Project '79 staff reviewed themes from the Tech Vision Summit, compared them with notes from our individual efforts, and collaborated to develop three initial goals for our use of instructional technology. Well-defined objectives would enable us to be clear about our purpose and "keep it in the forefront" (Lytle, 2010, p. 63).

Tact was key at this stage. While it's important for all kinds of leaders to discover and acknowledge the sensibilities of those they are supposed to lead, it's especially important for teacher leaders, who typically have little formal authority to enact change. At this time, staff readiness to explore classroom technology was diverse. One of our teachers was a pioneer in rethinking the possibilities of a tech-infused classroom, but at least one other was a fairly traditional lecturer who held that the prime role of teacher was content expert. Several of us were leery about being less familiar with many devices and platforms than our students. Over the course of several discussions, I pushed the opportunity to capitalize on students' knowledge of technology, adding that there would always be roles for adults to model question-posing and problem-framing for students. Also, while there were some "tech whizzes" in the class, that label definitely didn't apply to all our students! Most important, teachers bring to the table our knowledge of students' strengths and challenges. To get us started, we developed three non-radical goals for the use of classroom technology:

1. ***Communication.*** Students will develop skills related to electronic communication and collaboration, such as composing professional emails to arrange appointments with teachers for extra help and collaborating with peers through applications like Google Docs.
2. ***Research.*** Students will refine their ability to conduct online research, including understanding why a given source might be more or less trustworthy than another.
3. ***Organization.*** Students will develop a system for personal organization (note-taking, time management, keeping track of work) that makes sense for them.

AUTHORIZING STUDENTS TO EXPLORE

As I conceptualize this participatory inquiry in retrospect, it divides into two major phases. The first, reframing technology as an adaptive challenge, leaned heavily on the participation of Project '79 staff, who brought their experience, questions, and ideas to the fore. Students and other stakeholders mattered, but they effectively played minor roles in the first stages of rethinking classroom technology for teaching and learning. The second part is where we drew students deeper into the inquiry, authorizing them to explore with us.

Bring Your Own Device (BYOD)

Back at the conference table, Project '79 staff were pondering how to begin. We discussed the specifics of what students would require in order to start exploring these goals we called Communication, Research, and Personal Organization. Aware that we had no special funding to devote to the project, we chose the low-hanging fruit. In order to learn what resources were readily available, we surveyed students about what Internet-enabled devices they already owned. We decided to focus initially on that year's junior class (29 students) for several reasons: All students reported having access to a suitable device; research is a major curricular emphasis of junior year; as upperclassmen, the juniors were leaders within the Project '79 community who would be with us longer than our seniors; and the range of Android devices, iPhones, tablets, iPods, and laptops they intended to use would let us compare the effectiveness of various devices.

The next hurdle was policy. Mainly because of concerns about liability, no student in the district had a school email account or access to school Wi-Fi for all classes. Project '79 would need special permission for these. However, it's not always easy to get the attention of district personnel, who usually have many irons in the fire. My first strategy for "managing up" was what had proven reliable for me many times before: align my proposal with a preferred value of the school district. Technology was a current buzzword; Project '79 was trying to do something concrete and forward-thinking with tech; if it goes well, everybody looks good. (This rationale was basically how I influenced the assistant superintendent to attend the tech vision meeting.)

At this stage, unfortunately, district personnel were unresponsive, so I tried a tactic whose characterization among district administrators my building principal later described to me: "The word on the street is you've *gone rogue*." Because we needed to move expeditiously to get things going before the end of the school year, I reached out directly and invited three Board of Education members who were vocal proponents of technology to a meeting with Project '79 staff and students. Contacting Board members directly, I knew, was not often done, so I was not entirely surprised to find myself suddenly summoned to meet with the superintendent and assistant superintendent. Because they were both interested in resolving the matter quickly, I was able to arrange for Project '79 juniors to become the first students in the district to be granted school email accounts and access to the school Wi-Fi network for all their classes.

In return, we would gather data on what we learned, and make this information available to anyone interested in evaluating the effectiveness of our tech initiatives. I wanted tech data to be available for anyone interested in mixing things up at the high school, where some classrooms and hallways had posters warning "PHONES OFF, BRAINS ON. ANY QUESTIONS?" Most importantly for participatory inquiry, I wanted Project '79 students and staff to be able to learn together from our experiments.

Learning from BYOD

Six months after our students began using their devices in all classes, I asked them to reflect on their experience with BYOD and school-supplied email, as well as other tech platforms we were experimenting with at the time (Twitter, the microblog Tumblr, and the classroom platform Edmodo). Because the BYOD students were all in my English class, I deployed a supplemental essay question on my midterm exam to gather perceptions about each aspect of tech, as well as any suggestions. Influenced by data visualization guru Edward Tufte, my plan was to design a qualitative data display that would let everyone read and compare differing perceptions of how the exploration was going, and to pose new questions. The data display presented anonymous perceptions culled from exam essays, numbered for ease of reference in categories according to each platform, and subheadings according to each tech goal. There were general observations (e.g., "Made us feel trusted like adults—which is very important in education"); comments on the utility of devices for research and learning (e.g., "Being connected to the Internet has given me a knowledge base that surpasses every textbook in the school, allowing me to fact-check instantly"); responses about using devices to stay organized (e.g., "Note-taking is a little faster, and I'm able to read my notes"); and general concerns about tech ("With students who are already addicted to their phones, BYOD seems totally backwards"). Like many datasets, there were some contradictory indications, such as comments affirming vs. denying the efficacy of phones for school use. I believed it was very important for our students to contend with such ambiguities, because they are a part of life, with or without participatory inquiry!

I confess that I was hoping these students (now seniors) would really appreciate the work I invested to develop these displays as reflections of their perspectives, of their own voices as students. Before discussion, I explained my method of developing the data displays (e.g., how I notated similar responses), but also why I wanted them to be able to compare their classmates' perceptions about the tech initiative with their own. Reminding students that we were just getting started, I asked them to engage with this information not just for themselves at the start of their last semester of high school, but also for those who would follow. Despite my earnest pitch, the discussion was lackluster. Students noted a few obviously contradictory responses, sparred lightly on topics such as phone addiction and how to tactfully recommend Internet resources to their teachers, but no significant rethinking of teaching or learning occurred that day.

My next move was to ask students to take more of a leadership role and develop possible plans based on what they determined mattered most. The following week, we explored problem-framing. I assigned each participant to identify the most significant problem that they saw (a) reflected in the data and (b) corroborated by their own experience, in order to develop a formal proposal that would address this problem. Some students targeted the hazard of spending so much time looking at screens that they would not develop or refine social skills. Several discussed the difficulty of accessing school email via the clunky school website. One student suggested, "If there was an app that we could open straight from our phones' home screens, everyone would use it almost every day." Another made a compelling case that laptops should be the preferred device for school use because the "physical keyboard makes it much easier to type and laptops just have more of a business feel." He argued that, as more "personal" devices, phones "are used so much that checking social media is an instinct every time" you pick them up. Of the 29 proposals, I felt that only the argument for laptops and the plea to simplify school email really considered problems and possible solutions in nuanced ways. However, some of the students did seem gratified to be included as co-designers in our efforts to improve school.

Launching the Chromebook Pilot

As I've gained leadership experience, I've gotten better at sorting out which problems I should tackle, and which are best set for other people to solve. When an alumnus of the school contacted me to express his interest in funding a technology initiative, I immediately sought help from Jackie Spring, a more tech-experienced member of the faculty. I wanted her to take the lead in developing a concise roadmap for our tech vision with a set of benchmarks that would persuade our donor that we were serious about tracking the effectiveness of his potential investment in nearly 100 new Google Chromebooks, and guide a gradual transition in Project '79 classrooms from more conventional to more tech-infused, student-centered learning environments. (We chose Chromebooks after two students researched and compared a range of laptops.) Within a few weeks our roadmap was approved, and we had a check for 10 Chromebooks to get us started with a pilot group.

Project '79 staff and I determined that an application process would help us identify a core group of student leaders who were not only interested in having 24/7 access to a free computer but also committed to doing some trailblazing for us and other students in the high school. To encourage grade-level diversity, we opened the process to all four levels of Project '79 students. The application form reminded candidates of our tech goals and outlined our charge for students to explore sites and apps widely "to get a feel for what's out there and what we could be doing to improve teaching and learning." Selected applicants would become "go-to support people for teachers and students in learning how to use Chromebooks, and how to use them better." We stipulated expectations for students to keep asking: *Why do we use technology this way? How could we do it better? What else is out there? What if we tried . . . ?* The application asked them to demonstrate understanding of our expectations, to note their experience with tech, and to share their best current ideas about how Project '79 could take advantage of Chromebooks in the classroom. One applicant responded:

> The nice thing is that a Chromebook provides a single workstation. You're home, you're at school, you're out. I just want people to be able to work together in a more efficient manner. It's easy to lose paper, but put it on the cloud and it's always very accessible. I want to make sure everybody is always able to work without losing any progress.

Staff selected seven strong applications from about 18 completed by members of all four grades, a response rate of approximately 20%. As to the other three Chromebooks available at this stage, we decided that it would be wise to have several staff members learning how to use the new devices alongside the students.

Over the next several weeks, the Project '79 "pilots" (a name everybody felt captured the spirit of exploration we wanted students to embrace) took their charge seriously, often spending lunch and free periods conferring with each other and other Project '79 students about what they were discovering about the capabilities of this new tool. They experimented with different apps, did trouble-shooting with IT personnel to link our office printer to the Chromebooks, met with external tech experts, emailed network administrators with updates or requests to tweak network configurations, taught staff how to set up Google Classroom, presented updates to our parents group and our donor, and debated about the best platforms to use. Sometimes students stumbled as they experimented with how to impart a concept effectively. One pilot recalled asking a teacher, "Why don't you think about Google Classroom?" The teacher replied, "Because I have absolutely no idea what you're talking about." It was exciting to see students energized by the challenge, acting as teachers and influencers. Within months, our donor made it possible to provide Chromebooks to all Project '79 students. At the very end of the year, another pilot assumed the role of inquiring manager, including in his independent research project a survey of all Project '79 students who had been working with Chromebooks, so that he could make data-driven recommendations about next steps.

CONCLUSIONS

This story spins from three strands: leading a school program as a classroom teacher, instructional technology as an example of an adaptive challenge, and authorizing students to participate differently in school. With respect to teacher leadership, I coordinated this phase of technology inquiry as I tried to coordinate Project '79: inventing where I needed to, but more often setting problems to be solved by students, colleagues, and other stakeholders. In my view, the challenges of leading from the middle of an organization are outweighed by the creative possibilities for leadership of a small group of committed teachers by a colleague still teaching in a classroom. This model of teacher leadership is well worth considering, especially in schools that have sought to save money by eliminating supervisors' teaching responsibilities.

The adaptive challenge that prompted this inquiry remains an adaptive challenge. Our experiments allowed Project '79 to get started in thinking more deeply about how we could use technology to transform teaching and learning, but we didn't get all that far. Our pilots made many good discoveries, but they were primarily technical solutions. And what of our progress in using technology to shift to the kind of student-centered learning lab we dreamed about in our roadmap? As Jackie Spring, the former colleague who now leads Project '79, put it recently, "We're still stuck. What would be required to reach a new classroom paradigm is an uninstalling of the system we have had for generations. We're still at a crossroads with technology." Schools and other organizations will continue to contend with new technology, and the ways technology will continue to influence learning, work, and the rest of our lives. However, as Ali Michael (2015) observes, inquiry is not about finding straightforward answers, once and for all. Rather, it's about the process of seeking answers, "and being open to the idea that we might continue to learn the answers well after the time when we first needed to know them" (p. 36).

I kept inquiring as I was writing this chapter, and I reached out to several of the students who served as pilots, now all high school graduates. I discovered that our tech process had let them see themselves, and learning, in new ways. One former pilot recalled "experiencing education in a new mindset" and the value of being allowed to take learning into his own hands. Another loved getting "new eyes—student eyes—on the problem and seeing if there's another way to go about it." I like this comment especially, because it affirms the kinds of knowledge that students already bring with them to school but may not be aware they possess. Students may not have the lived experience or content knowledge that their teachers do, but they have a well of expertise related to how they learn and insights into how their peers might learn better, which educators could draw from if we invited students to participate more actively in the learning process and learned to listen to what they have to say about it. This confirmed my own experience as a teacher. In my classroom career of nearly 2 decades, I was observed by many supervisors and administrators. Yet, the most helpful feedback on my teaching that I received on a regular basis focused on the anonymous formative assessment from students that I solicited at the close of each marking period.

In any organization, enhanced agency given to underutilized participants can pay outsized dividends. In the case of Project '79, authorizing students meant inviting students to sit at the table, interpret data, identify problems, propose solutions, explore tech possibilities, and lead next steps. As one pilot said, "I was able to teach teachers some things that they wouldn't know how to teach us." Of course, it's not that students always know better than adults. What worked in our process was the *collaboration* of students and adults. "It was cool to be more than a student in the school. I think that everyone would agree that they were able to be *more than a student* for a time." The Project '79 Chromebook pilot who provided the title for this chapter said, "As only a sophomore, I felt like I was taking a leadership position—my first one." He has since served as a peer minister, formed a suicide-prevention group, and started a podcast on mental health. "My takeaway was [that] *it doesn't matter who you are, leaders can be anyone*."

Dewey (1938) might agree. He was unequivocal about the participation of students in the learning process:

> There is, I think, no point in the philosophy of progressive education which is sounder than its emphasis upon the importance of the participation of the learner in the formation of the purposes which direct his activities in the learning process, just as there is no defect in traditional education greater than its failure to secure the active cooperation of the pupil in construction of the purposes involved in his studying. (p. 67)

In our education program, we took our best shot at a tough problem together. I believe that similar experiments could yield positive results for any kind of organization, not to mention the individual members. As one Project '79 pilot put it, "Instead of 'This is the way we've been doing it' and 'This is how we're going to do it,' we were like, 'How can we get at this together?' . . . That was refreshing."

REFERENCES

Cook-Sather, A. (2002). Authorizing students' perspectives: Toward trust, dialogue, and change in education. *Educational Researcher, 31*(4), 3–14.

Davidson, C. N. (2011). *Now you see it: How the brain science of attention will transform the way we live, work, and learn.* New York, NY: Viking.

Dewey, J. (1938). *Experience and education.* New York, NY: Touchstone.

Heifetz, R. A., & Linsky, M. (2002). *Leadership on the line: Staying alive through the dangers of leading.* Cambridge, MA: Harvard Business School.

Lytle, J. H. (2010). *Working for kids: Education leadership as inquiry and invention.* Latham, MD: Rowman & Littlefield.

Michael, A. (2015). *Raising race questions: Whiteness & inquiry in education.* New York, NY: Teachers College Press.

Part II

COLLABORATING WITH TEACHERS AND THE SCHOOL COMMUNITY

CHAPTER 5

Deepening Engagement in the Everyday

The Collective Responsibility for Seeing All Children

Patricia Cruice

Having spent 27 years in public education, ***Patricia Cruice*** has served as the principal of a K–8 school for the past 9 years. She initially embraced an inquiry stance as a beginning teacher through her studies at the Prospect Center and engagement with the Philadelphia Teachers' Learning Cooperative. As a teacher, a mentor, and a member of the Federation of Teachers' Executive Board for 10 years, she has advocated for an approach to teaching that links teacher and student learning. Cruice earned her doctorate in educational leadership from the University of Pennsylvania, her master's degree in education and certification in elementary education from Antioch/New England Graduate School, a master's from Lehigh University in educational administration, and her BA from Temple University.

Teachers' everyday talk about students' capacities has been heavily influenced by the narrowing of the curriculum resulting from the "teach to the test" dynamic in urban schools. Additionally, standardized tests as required by NCLB and ESSA have become a largely punitive measure rather than the diagnostic tool they were originally intended to be, and educator evaluations are increasingly tied to student test scores. From my perspective, punishment of both the most vulnerable students and the teachers who teach them is the overriding outcome of this standardized testing frenzy. In the wake of this shift in curriculum, instruction, and assessment, students are often reduced to such labels as "at risk" or "bubble kids" (those who have scored on the cusp of basic/proficient and are targeted for intervention in order to "push" them over the line). Standardized test data crowd out other, more nuanced descriptions. To reduce the representation of a child as learner to that of a test score is extremely limiting and problematic.

The pressures on educators to perform and conform to the larger policy and cultural forces impacting K–12 public schools are most acutely experienced in urban districts where the latest "teacher-proof" packaged curriculum is rolled out onto beleaguered teachers and students. Interrupting the rush to label children can be difficult. Limited by the routines of school, where "short-hand" language is traded among harried teachers and educational leaders, educators need a space to pause and examine the assumptions undergirding the deficit language that is used to define the capacities of large groups of children. I regard creating the context for teachers to work together using more complex and richer descriptions of children as a primary task of urban educational leaders, driven by a central question beyond the testing profile: How *do* we know our students, and how *can* we know them better?

LEARNING TO TEACH, LEARNING TO INQUIRE

In many respects, I began my career in education as an accidental teacher. With an undergraduate liberal arts degree and not a single course in education, I entered a classroom in a small Catholic school in a poor, minority neighborhood in Philadelphia. Armed with little more than a strong belief in the social justice message of the progressive Catholic left movement, I leapt into my work as the 4th-grade teacher. While my own formal K–12 education in working-class Catholic schools in the city in many ways replicated the dominant ideology, my perspective was enlarged by teachers dedicated to the emancipatory message of liberation theology. Hence, it was in the dialectical nature of the educational process that, despite being situated within a structure designed to ensure my obedience, I began to question and reframe my experiences as both a learner and beginning teacher.

Despite this emergent inclination to inquire, I soon learned that I was ill-prepared for the task of teaching children, particularly the children of a marginalized community of which I was not a part. I was unaware of what I did not know regarding the centrality of the student in the teaching and learning endeavor. Fortunately, a friend introduced me to the Philadelphia Teachers' Learning Cooperative (PTLC) and, in the shelter of a circle of veteran teachers from both public and private schools, I began to learn how to channel my passion in ways that might actually serve my students. It was within this caring group that I was first exposed to the Prospect Center Descriptive Processes (PDP) (Carini, 1979; Carini & Himley, 2010; Himley, 2002; Himley & Carini, 2000) and experienced their power to make the intricacies of teaching and learning visible through a phenomenological perspective. The valuing of humanness in all its complexity that is at the heart of the Descriptive Processes aligned with my deepest beliefs about the ultimate integrity and uniqueness of all persons.

I completed certification studies at the Prospect Center for Education and Research teacher education program and embarked on a career in the School District of Philadelphia. Though young and idealistic, I knew the strength of the collective would be necessary to sustain me in the work. If it weren't for the fellowship found in those regular Thursday afternoon meetings of the PTLC, I doubt I would be where I am now in my role as principal, investigating the way disciplined collaborative reflection can inform the work of teachers. This approach to inquiry was forged in my early years with PTLC, reinforced through fruitful study at the Prospect Center, and further supported through involvement in the Philadelphia Writing Project and the Penn Literacy Network. It has served as necessary ballast while I established myself as a teacher and leader in this large urban district.

From all that I now carry with me into the principalship, I believe that learning to take an inquiry stance, as manifested many years ago in the PDP, has the power to alter the way we think about children (see Cruice, 2014). As principal-teacher, I seek to influence a change in the discourse about students and their "deficits." I want to highlight the centrality of teachers' collective abilities to describe students in all their complexity. And as principal-teacher specifically, I ask myself: How can I support the generation of teachers' local knowledge in order to support the larger quest for educational opportunity for all children?

LEARNING TO DESCRIBE

Engaging with the Prospect Descriptive Processes calls to the forefront key assumptions about what it means to bring discipline to description and commitment to collaborative inquiry. Trust and time are necessary. Relational trust is the foundation upon which collective responsibility is built (Bryk & Schneider, 2002). The nature of the processes invites teachers' collaborative inquiry into practice: describing students in rich detail without critique or evaluation, learning and supporting the practice of active listening (withholding comments until a designated time), and embracing a strengths-based approach to instruction.

The Descriptive Processes were developed at The Prospect School in North Bennington, Vermont (Carini, 1979), and create structures that invite connections between and among teachers meeting in groups to discuss the work of teaching and learning. Enacting the descriptive processes, teachers connect around and through the questions that surface in their daily work with children. The processes, and in particular one called The Descriptive Review of a Child, are not intended to solve a problem or change a child. Instead, they make visible the complexities of individual students, surfacing particular strengths and interests. We learn from and with each other.

Keeping the child at the center of teachers' descriptions and reflection serves to ground teachers in meaningful work. This approach helps to counter the condition of cynicism and isolation prevalent in underfunded urban public schools by inspiring teachers to value their ability to observe children in order to support student growth. When difficulties arise in the teaching/learning dynamic, a descriptive review can serve as a reset or reboot.

The format of the descriptive review process is one way for teachers to recognize how much they already know and understand about the child. It is meant, also, to add to this knowledge base to enhance a teacher's approach to the child's learning. During a pre-conference, the presenting teacher, in collaboration with the chairperson/facilitator, determines a focusing question that frames the description. As the instructional leader of the school, I played the role of chair in these reviews. In the pre-conference, the focusing question should be rich with the potential to encourage deep deliberation. In my school, the Descriptive Review of the Child was structured by a set of headings serving as prompts for a teacher's recollections that, when taken together, form a picture of the child to set the stage for the teacher-to-teacher dialogue that follows.

To familiarize the reader with the interpretive framework of the process, I provide a brief account of the headings that the presenting teacher prepares prior to the day of the descriptive review:

1. ***Physical Presence and Gesture:*** Starting with a description of the child's *physical presence and gesture*, the presenting teacher strives to convey the child's size and build, and also the amount of space the child occupies, characteristic rhythm and gestures, inflections in voice, and level of energy. A description of the child's characteristic temperament and range of emotions and the way in which feelings are expressed also fall under this heading.
2. ***Relationships with Children and Adults:*** Does the child have friends? Characterizing those attachments, along with an investigation into the child's interpersonal connections with others, falls under the heading of *relationships with children and adults.* Teasing out the details of how the child's interactions with others vary or are influenced by the amount or intensity of day-to-day contact are some of the threads to follow when documenting under this heading.
3. ***Activities and Interests:*** This is the place where a teacher speaks to the child's preferred *activities and interests*. The greater the detail of this section, the more fruitful the descriptive review. Speaking to the child's engagement with objects and ideas relies upon a teacher's capacity to observe what has a strong appeal to the child.
4. ***Formal Learning:*** In the final section, *formal learning*, the presenting teacher shares her observations of the child's experiences with subjects taught in school. Examples of the child's approach to a new subject or process help to portray the child as a thinker and learner in the school setting.

I am describing the content of the review in some detail so that the unique valence of this process is made apparent. After this detailed description by the presenting teacher, which lasts approximately 20 minutes during which all of the other participants are silent, listen and take notes, and do not interrupt the presentation, the chairperson offers a *summary of the dominant themes and patterns* and then restates the focusing question. A round of *clarifying/probing questions* from participants directed to the presenter generates new information which, in turn, adds to the fullness of the description of the child. Sitting in a circle, teachers are urged to set aside conventional labels, categories, and judgments. The chairperson/facilitator then shares another *summary of the presentation,* reiterating/adding dominant themes and patterns, along with a restatement of the focusing question. The discussion that follows provides an opportunity for participants to share what they have heard and to offer suggestions and recommendations. The presenting teacher, at this time, may choose to comment, or not, on anything she has heard. The *presenter's response* is then followed by a *debriefing* of the process by all involved, addressing the question: How did this process serve us as a faculty?

Finding a way to import this practice into the busy routine of school days was the challenge I took up with the leadership team at my elementary school. We set about to structure our time in a way that would allow teachers to meet for extended time in what we called Small Learning Communities (SLC) during the course of the school day. Professional development monies from the Title 1 budget funded substitute teacher service for a total of 5 days throughout the school year, and teachers appreciated being "just down the hall" from their classrooms.

As the instructional leader and chairperson, what I learned from facilitating groups of teachers using the Prospect Descriptive Processes at my school is that when dialogue is supported with requisite levels of trust, honesty, and mutuality, occurs over time, and follows established, specific procedures, teacher talk (even in early conversations) can become a powerful form of oral inquiry capable of producing understanding and wisdom about the work of teaching and learning. Multiple perspectives can be captured in the processes of oral inquiry, informing problem posing and solving. The dialogue is knowledge-producing; that is, disciplined dialogue that follows specific, theoretically-grounded structures prompts rich and often startling insights.

Importantly, teachers can come to recognize aspects of all children in the descriptive review of the presented child, while the act of recognizing the uniqueness of each child reaffirms the valuing of all children. Built upon the belief in human capacity, widely distributed, the Descriptive Processes can foster genuine deliberation that, in turn, supports democratic action.

SEEING STUDENTS: TEACHERS AS GENERATORS OF KNOWLEDGE

To these gatherings, teachers brought their questions about children and a willingness to engage in the inquiry. The SLC meetings became a space for the joint construction of knowledge, with presenting teachers driven by a burning question and their colleagues immersed in the work of active listening and rich description. Structured dialogue, as a way of knowing better or differently, supported our work as educators. In order to see their students in all their complexity, teachers were given the opportunity to examine a much richer and wider array of available data than test scores, report card grades, or other typical summative classroom assessments.

For teachers, adopting an inquiry stance, which the descriptive processes facilitate, is at once simple and complex. Deepening engagement with the work of everyday teaching begins with a willingness to pause and reflect, and is refined throughout one's teaching career. The two vignettes that follow are partial descriptions of what happened at our first extended SLC meeting. Most teachers had no prior experience with the Prospect Descriptive Processes, and yet the transcripts revealed an embracing of the process that tapped into the local knowledge that teachers carry within themselves.

"She is a girl full of ideas."

The Lower School SLC was a group of primary grade teachers (K–4) and consisted of women, all of whom are mothers and many of whom have mutual connections outside of school. This first meeting featured the presentation of a second-grade student, Jenna, by her teacher, Nissa,* who is a member of The Philadelphia Writing Project (PhilWP) and had some prior experience with the Prospect Descriptive Processes. I decided to serve as the chair/facilitator in these early meetings because the processes were so new to most teachers.

In preparation for the first descriptive review, we engaged in a *Reflection on a Word*, a descriptive process that often precedes descriptive reviews. The activity of reflecting on a word is not meant to arrive at a narrow definition. Rather, each participant surveys their memories for recollections of phrases, words, or images that the word conjures up. Teachers contribute their immediate associations and this expansive exploration of what the word connotes becomes shared knowledge. This discussion primes the participants for the descriptive review. The chair and presenter collaborate on the selection of word or phrase, seeking to add depth to the discussion in the descriptive review to follow.

To maximize our time together, we engaged in a reflection on a word with the word *visibility* during the 45-minute SLC meeting the week before the presentation. Visibility was described from "clear" to "cloudy," "shallow" to "deep"; the idea that to be seen, *somebody* has to see *you* was also voiced. I summarized the multiple associations the Lower School SLC had with the word "*visibility*" and transcribed them onto poster-sized paper, which was left hanging for the week that preceded the descriptive review. The words, phrases, and images conjured up during the reflection marinated, if you will, in the teachers' minds prior to the day of the descriptive review.

Nissa's focusing question set the context for the description that followed: "How can I help Jenna, who is new to the school, develop an outlook that allows her to be present to the immediate process of learning without needing to have the 'right answer,' and to embrace a growth stance"? The next 90 minutes was devoted to a rich description of the student by the presenting teacher, followed by wonderings and probing questions by the participating teachers. Nissa's description of the

*Pseudonyms are used to protect the confidentiality of both teachers and students.

child as a "loquacious, bubbly" girl was replete with examples of the child's presence in Nissa's classroom: how the child turns a phrase, her characteristic gestures, her relationship with others, and the nature of Jenna's sense-making.

Nissa began by explaining that Jenna arrived at this new school because a nearby elementary school was closed. Jenna's mother had shared with her teacher concern over difficulties that Jenna encountered getting to her new school. Jenna had expressed sadness regarding activities she missed as a result of absences, and Nissa added that, particularly with academic subjects, Jenna often had to "play catch-up." Nissa postulated that Jenna experienced a feeling of "dissonance" each time she re-entered the classroom after being absent.

Regarding *Relationships with Adults and Children*, Nissa shared positive comments she had received from specialist teachers concerning Jenna. These remarks represented the child's tenor as that of a young girl with an insatiable interest in learning, which was evidenced by a willingness to contribute suggestions in class. Nissa amusingly described how she had "stepped up" her classroom's birthday celebration tradition after Jenna posed questions such as "Where's the crown?" Nissa asserted that Jenna's penchant for enhancement is one of her strengths: "She is a girl full of ideas; she is not shy at all." In turning to *Formal Learning*, Nissa portrayed a girl who is a deep thinker, can analyze, and was told by her previous teacher that she was "gifted." Nissa described how Jenna responds to feedback that counters what Jenna may have been accustomed to receiving in the past. Jenna resisted making any revisions to her work.

At the end of the descriptive review, one teacher commented on the value of listening to Nissa uninterrupted as being able to "actually get to the whole story." This same teacher said she realized that "you cannot really help somebody until you know the whole story" and observed how the perceptive and richly detailed information shared was an example of what's possible when teachers are given time to meet and an agenda that foregrounds children in all their complexity. Another teacher highlighted how the process challenged her to think of her class of 28 students not as a single entity but rather as a group of unique individuals, each deserving of a personal approach by the teacher.

In talking about what this process had afforded her, Nissa shared an image of a sculptor chiseling away to unveil what can be seen beneath. Her response to her colleagues' thoughts braided her observations with the comments of other teachers and made palpable the possibilities of caring for all the students new to our school, not just Jenna. One participant also articulated how the process stimulated reflection on particular students in her own classroom and attributed this, in part, to Nissa's full and detailed presentation. In addition, she said, "I can, kind of, start thinking of my kids in a different way. Instead of just saying they are not growing . . . it is now . . . Well, why is that?" This beginning teacher thus grappled with what it would mean to allow students to use more than one way to learn from lessons that she created.

Through the experience of the Descriptive Review, the teachers not only had an opportunity to think about and wrestle with their own challenges, but they also practiced a mode of generative discussion previously not experienced in teacher-to-teacher group conversations. Teachers were able to consider multiple possibilities, to employ ways of reasoning that did not degenerate into a rhetoric of conclusions. This is the narrative of inquiry: attentive, thoughtful discussion that can advance professional learning.

In the questioning phase of the process, teachers framed interpretations as conjectures, not as assertions. To have a growing awareness of what it means *to learn from teaching*, to regard the practice of teaching as something to study so as to become better, is more generative than simply thinking of oneself as an "experienced" teacher.

An inquiry stance is, at heart, a willingness to embrace a deliberative uncertainty in and about one's practice: to question, consider, and analyze alternatives. Teachers' willingness to remain in the question—to fight the urge to rush to conclusions—is supported by the structure of the Descriptive Review. Possibilities generated during the review opened up a vista for Nissa to investigate, as she contemplated the ways in which Jenna embraced her learning and claimed her place in the classroom.

"Derrick is like a turtle; he definitely hides."

The Upper School's (5–8) SLC also had previously participated in the process of *Reflection on a Word*. We used the same word, *visibility*, and the reflection was reviewed prior to the Descriptive Review of Derrick, a student in Amy's 8th-grade classroom. The focusing question was shared: "How can I honor Derrick's need for autonomy while also providing the supports that will facilitate his mastery of academic material that challenges him?"

Derrick begins his school day in Amy's 8th-grade homeroom. Amy is also Derrick's math and science teacher. Amy's description of Derrick included reference to his *stance and gesture* in the classroom. She described him as becoming "visibly uncomfortable" whenever Amy tried to approach him to offer additional one-to-one support. Derrick shook his head and/or hands in signals that he didn't need any help whenever Amy circled the class offering to help students individually. In describing Derrick's *relationships with children and adults*, Amy spoke of Derrick's ease and self-confidence in social relations with peers. He seemed to be a leader within his social circle and appeared to be well liked. Regarding *activities and interests*, Amy reported that Derrick played basketball outside of school and during recess. She described him as a student who enjoyed the hands-on activities of science labs. In reference to *formal learning*, Amy noted that Derrick completed both class work and homework and commented on the care with which Derrick took to produce a pleasing "final product." Amy remarked that during class discussions, Derrick appeared to want to blend in or "hide."

As the chair, I provided a brief summary highlighting dominant themes and patterns and then invited Linda, Derrick's English and social studies teacher, to add her perspective to the evolving picture of Derrick. Lucy and Angela, the music and graphic arts teachers, respectively, contributed their perspectives on Derrick as well. These multiple perspectives, from different subject area teachers, illustrated how he adopted different ways of participating in various classrooms and added to the portrait of the child.

I then moved the group to clarifying and/or probing questions from participants. In responding to a question, Amy utilized the image of a turtle to describe how Derrick can duck down in his desk whenever Amy approaches during independent work time. "Derrick is like a turtle; he definitely hides." The teachers discussed the importance of focusing on a student like Derrick to ensure that he doesn't become "a kid who falls between the cracks."

As the Chair, I summarized the themes that arose from the questioning phase and moved to a sharing of words/phrases/images that stood out to the teachers. For example, Derrick's self-esteem was mentioned. The tendency for educators to "label" students is deeply ingrained; at this point in the descriptive review, teacher talk lapsed into short-hand language to describe some of his perceived deficits. Just as quickly, though, the graphic arts teacher offered a more expansive insight, describing Derrick as the idea man who "doesn't do details but has big-picture thinking."

Recommendations offered to Amy tapped into other teachers' prior experiences in their own classrooms, leveraged Derrick's strengths to assist the teaching/learning process, and opened up vistas for Amy to explore. The *debrief of the process* among the Upper School teachers included comments on the value of looking closely at a student who can often be "invisible" in the classroom. Several teachers shared that they were reminded of a child in their own class. Teachers also remarked that the chance to sit with colleagues for an extended time, slowly describing one student, was extremely helpful and thought-provoking for their own classroom practice and stimulated more nuanced observations of their own students.

From my experience engaging with teachers in the process of Descriptive Review, even in their first efforts, I saw how teachers' frameworks and language about students can become richer and more nuanced through systematic, sustained (and slow) oral inquiry. Over time, the obvious complexity of children serves to open up avenues to further connections and possibilities.

THE STRUGGLE TO REFRAME

As these two examples demonstrate, the Descriptive Processes afford a disciplined approach to teacher talk that resists labeling children, challenges teachers to refrain from judgment, and generally slows down the rush for easy "answers" to the many complex challenges that teachers face daily. They invite teachers to play out their natural curiosity about student learning and their own learning as well, across the lifespan of teaching experience. The process gives teachers unusual access to each other's ideas, experiences, and ways of knowing through structured, disciplined discourse (for a related format, see also National School Reform Faculty [NSRF] adaptation of the Prospect Descriptive Review).

Teachers need space to interrogate their (often unarticulated) beliefs in the shelter of a group in which relational trust has been established. I saw how, absent the need to "defend" one's position in this era of teacher "accountability" and blaming, most teachers were drawn to examine their thinking, revise their analyses, and reframe their approach to problems of practice. Over time, with trust deepening, teachers are able to push each other's thinking and to examine previously unquestioned assumptions. In the course of just one year, I observed how the generative nature of disciplined oral inquiry can replenish teachers' intellectual resources, sharpen their observational skills, and tap into a fundamental capacity of most (if not all) teachers to become more aware of the complexity and uniqueness of all children.

This is inquiry as action, where the serious work of observation is coupled with ideas for moving forward. Whether with regard to a child, a child's piece of artwork or writing, or a particular problem of practice, attending to the disciplined work of careful description liberates a teacher from the limits of routinized thinking.

This collective responsibility for student learning is also sustained when teaching becomes less a private matter and more of a joint venture. The Descriptive Processes de-privatize teaching practice in a way that honors teacher knowledge while also inviting teachers to stretch their understanding of the child, work, or issue through disciplined description. Cultivating a culture of reflection and inquiry is one outcome of engaging with the Descriptive Processes that supports a collective responsibility for student learning.

LEADING AS A FORM OF INQUIRY

From my experience as a principal facilitating inquiry with teachers, a leader's role in creating the space to enable a disciplined approach to description and sustained conversation among colleagues is critical. Posing open-ended questions contrasts with the dominant practice of identifying learning gaps, of selecting an intervention from the approved list of research-based interventions, and of evaluating effectiveness through standardized testing. This kind of inquiry work interrupts the familiar or expected responses with the goal of deepening and widening all teachers' insight into teaching and learning.

Our experience using these approaches to better understand our students is ongoing, with fits and starts. For a leader grounded in inquiry, the inevitable messiness requires steadiness and faith in the process. Holding this cognitive dissonance is a key task of one who is leading from an inquiry stance. Space needs to be made for teachers to explore different voices and a different perspective from what they have experienced as "collaborative learning" in the past. When divergent voices are heard, the issue of "power" inevitably surfaces and can be scrutinized, and inquiry can shift power. When leaders create space for such discourse, belief systems can be safely questioned and examined. The act of examining and re-examining allows leaders and teachers to expand and complicate the meanings of what on the surface has appeared to be common understanding.

Looking back on this first year-long exploration of what it means to take an inquiry stance on our daily work at our elementary school, I see that the space created in the busy schedule of an urban public school allowed for an aura of possibility. Teachers engaged in an activity that held the child at the center of their work as educators and experienced firsthand a new way of looking at children and their work—coming to understand how such an examination can shed significant light on their practice as teachers. Serving as the principal, as one whose leadership stance is fundamentally committed to inquiring *with* teachers, I entered this endeavor yearning to create a space for faculty to work together in new ways. Although I had to conquer logistical challenges such as scheduling and teacher compensation, I believed deeply that school-wide engagement with the Descriptive Processes would provoke shifts in teacher thinking, challenge assumptions and beliefs, and generate adaptive change that supports learning.

Creating positive, permanent shifts in educator practice through the adoption of an inquiry stance requires sustained effort and concentration and remains a foundational aspiration of my leadership. The work of leading in the classroom or from the principal's desk involves by necessity the mastery of daily non-trivial tasks. However, doing the same thing over and over can lead one to believe that progress is occurring. Simply gaining experience does not necessarily translate to getting better. Teaching, at times, can devolve into mindless activity, where small errors are missed and daily opportunities for improvement are overlooked.

To counter this aspect of daily living in an elementary school, as a leader, I structure opportunities for teachers to embrace inquiry, to pause, to interrogate their assumptions. This is deliberative practice that is purposeful and systematic. It is focused attention. Looking at problems of practice through the lens of one of the Prospect Descriptive Processes uncovers personal and professional resources that can liberate educators from unexamined viewpoints and deepen the learning of students, teachers, *and* principals.

Urban public schooling is not built for authentic educator inquiry. A lasting institutional implementation of extended SLC meetings has proved to be elusive. However, for everyday teaching to be transformed by the praxis of observing and describing called for in Descriptive Reviews, time and practice are needed. To become significantly better at anything, it helps to fall in love with the process of doing it. At a critical juncture early in my career, I was taken by how the Descriptive Processes helped me gain insights into my students and my teaching, so I made the weekly trek to the revolving location of the Philadelphia Teachers' Learning Cooperative.

While instituting weekly extended-time SLCs has not been possible, the times we were able to engage with the Descriptive Processes fostered a kind of new professional discourse among teachers that visitors to the school have often remarked upon. I believe the nurturing of inquiring attitudes in teachers is necessary if we are to meet the needs of all students and go beyond relying on reductive labels and assumed limitations of children's capacities. In this era of data-driven instruction, it should not go unnoticed that Descriptive Reviews are a mode of formative assessment and provide data about the learning and growth of students. Teachers must shift from a focus on teaching students "what we know" to "how we come to know." An inquiry stance is a catalyst for change and growth in our classrooms. Learning opportunities such as the Descriptive Processes support teachers as they strive to answer the question, "How do we *know* our students and how can we know them better?"

REFERENCES

Bryk, A. S., & Schneider, B. (2002). *Trust in schools: A core resource for improvement.* New York, NY: Russell Sage Foundation.

Carini, P. F. (1979). The art of seeing and the visibility of the person. *North Dakota Study Group on Evaluation.* Grand Forks, ND: University of North Dakota.

Carini, P. F., & Himley, M. (2010). *Jenny's story: Taking the long view of the child.* New York, NY: Teachers College Press.

Cruice, P. A. (2014). *Teacher inquiry in small learning communities: Using the Prospect Center Descriptive Processes* (Doctoral dissertation). Retrieved from ProQuest Dissertations & Theses Database. (UMI No. 3635734).

Himley, M. (2002). *Prospect's Descriptive Processes: The child, the art of teaching & the classroom and the school.* North Bennington, VT: The Prospect Center.

Himley, M., & Carini, P. F. (2000). *From another angle: Children's strengths and school standards.* New York, NY: Teachers College Press.

CHAPTER 6

School as a Community of Inquiry

Noah Tennant

Noah Tennant is the CEO of Boys' Latin of Philadelphia Charter School. Boys' Latin is intentionally designed as a college preparatory school for boys from inner-city neighborhoods and has received national recognition for its success in preparing students for college entrance and completion. Prior to his appointment as CEO, Tennant served as the principal of Boys' Latin and was previously a teacher and administrator in suburban New Jersey schools. He earned his doctorate in educational leadership from the University of Pennsylvania, a master's degree from Teachers College, Columbia University, and his bachelor's degree from the University of Delaware.

Our school's maxim—*Every man is the architect of his own fortune*—is intended to instill a sense of purpose and vision. We seek to engage our students in regular, ongoing conversations about their roles and destinies in life. Their daily pledge, recited each morning, declares education to be their *birthright*. We want them to identify as scholars. We want them to feel an individual and collective responsibility to themselves and those who follow. We want them to embrace the legacy of our school as it existed before their arrival, and to consider how it will exist for future students. So a student assembly that focused on the cultural touchstones of today's generation, contrasted with those of past generations, aligned with our goals of teaching students about the evolution of thinking, style, and beliefs. Seeking to prompt reflection among our students, we intended the assembly to generate discussion about the value of learning others' points of view. We wanted to engage students in the challenging task of discerning which core character traits and attributes remain true consistently throughout time, versus those that change and bend.

The assembly consisted of a panel comprised of both staff and students discussing a series of images. The staff on the panel varied in race, gender, and age. Likewise, the topics the panel discussed varied. They began by discussing fashion, commenting on images of today's youth (i.e., skinny jeans) and yesterday's youth (i.e., baggy jeans). Next, the panel explored the word "nigger" and the meanings of, use of, and reactions toward the word by different individuals and different age groups over time. But it was the final image that prompted a deep split among and a surprising reaction from students. Projected on the screen was an image of Bill Cosby. Presenters hoped the image would evoke the notion of a fallen hero—a man who once represented wholesome goodness, America's Dad, but who was now seen as an alleged predator and rapist.

Unexpectedly, however, the student reaction did not align with the presenters' narrative. Students abruptly and loudly endorsed Bill Cosby. They pronounced his innocence. They defended him. They expressed that he, Cosby, was the victim—a victim of a racist media and money-seeking women. The assembly devolved into students shouting their opinions, and the adult leaders did not re-establish order. No one balanced the emotional expressions and outrage of the students with counterpoints. No one called for rational and respectful sharing. One student who did attempt to express an alternative point of view was shouted down and dismissed by his classmates. The faculty and students present who disagreed with this point of view were intimidated into silence. That is where the assembly ended.

OUR SCHOOL

Boys' Latin of Philadelphia strives to prepare boys for success in college. This school was founded because there were few options for students in the City of Philadelphia who wanted to attend a college-preparatory school. The schools that many students in our surrounding community were attending had a poor track record of college matriculation and college graduation. Boys' Latin was created with the express purpose of increasing the college graduation rates for Philadelphia students, specifically black males. Doing so was imperative. It expressed the ethics of properly serving students and safeguarding the welfare and posterity of an entire community. Our founders believed that if we gave students a strong education, a safe place to learn, and a dedicated faculty, they would achieve the same success as children in the adjoining suburbs.

I am a proud principal because we are achieving our mission. Our students are graduating from high school at a rate of 95%, compared to the 45% overall graduation rate of boys of color in our city. They are matriculating into college at a rate of 84%, compared to the 27% rate of boys of color in our city. Even more importantly, they are persisting into their second year of college at a rate of 67%, a rate nearly four times greater than that of boys of color in Philadelphia. Results show that our students are gaining and leveraging the academic skills necessary for success in college. Furthermore, they are exhibiting the non-traditional academic skills of grit and resilience necessary to navigate the world of post-secondary education.

LEADERSHIP IN TIMES OF STRUGGLE

I was not present for the assembly. All of my learning about the events happened after the fact; however, I did not have to solicit the accounts. When I returned to the high school (from the administrative offices), I had emails waiting for me and a queue of people at my office door. I spent time talking to every teacher who wanted to share their frustrations. I met with them individually. I met with them in groups. I shaped a team of teacher leaders to help me learn more and help our organization learn more. This group became a sounding board for others and an advisory team for me. Over the weeks that followed, this team helped plan the whole-faculty discussions and workshops that ensued.

Meanwhile, the first student I talked to was the one who attempted to speak up for the marginalized during the assembly but who was shut down. I met with him in my office, and I thanked him for his courage and voice. We went on to discuss the dynamics of the student body that he believed led to the division and frustration. He cited students' immaturity, their mob mentality, and their inability to think independently. He lamented their inability to interpret circumstances through their own lenses (based on the healthy relationships they had with their moms and their sisters and their teachers) rather than through the lens of social media.

Other students' reactions were varied. Some stood by their viewpoints. Some expressed blatant misogyny. But many expressed drastically different views in the "isolation" of my office than they had in the public forum of the assembly. They acknowledged, privately, that they believed Cosby to be guilty, and they offered apologies for what they understood to be disrespectful behavior toward others in the room during the assembly. It's unclear if this was their true thinking or a confession given under duress while sitting with the school principal.

Through these conversations I learned that there is a considerable difference between being *silent* and being *silenced*. Though there were many adults in the room during the assembly, their voices were suffocated. The surprise of the moment and the disappointment they felt sucked away their ability to respond in the moment. Despite their demonstrated strength, convictions, and authority, even they were silenced when it came to their core beliefs being dismissed so flippantly by the students they loved.

Finally, I learned that we as a faculty team had a great deal of work to do. While our common heart for our students brought us together, we were riddled with division. We were strong at capitalizing on our commonalities, but we did not know how to bridge our differences. We did not know how to be allies for one another.

We decided to first do some work as a faculty, as a team of adults. We thought it important to do this as a first step before addressing the situation with students. The team of teacher leaders and I forged this direction. It came from our need for healing. Our team was divided. We needed to look inward as a team and address our own dysfunction before we stood a chance of trying to address the situation with students. Fingers were pointing. There was no trust, and we needed to build that back up.

I knew that I must act quickly to heal the wounds caused by the assembly and to restore that faith. As a male, leading from an inquiry stance in this moment was born of necessity. But the frustrated faculty, many of whom were female and White, and reflective of the demographics of Cosby's alleged victims, were cut deeply by these events in ways that I needed to better understand.

Therefore, I sought their counsel and together we collectively launched a series of discussions designed to re-forge our community and empower us as adults to better prepare students for the world beyond our high school doors. This started with some challenging reflections, considerations, and questions about us, our students, and our community.

We decided to bring in outside consultants because so much of the matter was emotional and personal. We thought the objectivity of an outsider would be helpful. We also thought that having Boys' Latin leadership facilitate the sessions would undermine the message that ALL of us had much to learn.

I also believed that it would be a time for leadership, especially me, to be in the mindset of listening and learning rather than talking. Institutionally, we had to acknowledge our areas for growth and embrace the reality that our experiences are different—based on the many and varied traits that make us different—and acknowledge that our differences drastically impact how we experience Boys' Latin.

Who Am I, and Who Are We to Define the Ideal of Manhood for Our Students?

I am a Black man and a school leader. The formal authority of my position and my demographics gave me confidence in my ability to define these issues of manhood for our all-male, 99% Black, student body. But I also live in the New Jersey suburbs and needed to question whether my blackness and my gender fully qualified me to be the arbiter of manhood for my students in West Philadelphia. I had to recognize the potential limitations of my understanding of who these students needed to be as men, recognizing that who I need to be as a man in my world may be different from who they need to be in theirs. In addition, our school faculty and staff are not representative of the student body. Comprised of 56% women and 44% men, it is also largely White. Only 7 of the 23 male teachers represent historically under-represented groups, and only 6 of the 29 female teachers represent historically under-represented groups. We had a responsibility to be mindful of how our identities presented limits on what we could impose on the identity of our students.

Who Are Students Asked to Be While at Our School? Who Are They Asked to Be on Their Way to and from Our School?

Dressed in button-down shirts and ties, with navy blazers displaying the Boys' Latin crest, our students look sharp. They are a sight to behold—not just high-caliber thinkers, but also the perfect image of scholarly aspirations. I remember, though, my early observations of them during afternoon dismissal time. I watched students relegate their blazers to their lockers as soon as the final bell rang. They covered their ties with a hoodie, and they swapped their oxford shoes for boots or sneakers. I wondered why. I had hoped they would proudly wear their school uniforms home. I wanted them to be agents of Boys' Latin as they left the school, traveled public transit, and walked the neighborhoods. I wanted them to be symbols of the transcendent place that was our school.

I soon realized why they could not, when I had to visit the hospital to check on a student. Marcus S.*—a slender, deep-thinking, and friendly sophomore—had been struck with a blunt object as he walked home from his extracurricular activities. I learned how our students were periodically attacked by others in the nearby neighborhoods. Being a Boys' Latin student meant being the recipient of threats and harassment. Our students' lofty collegiate goals made them targets to others who—because of resentment, jealousy, anger, their own failures, or greed—did not want them to succeed.

It became clear to me that the kind of man we were asking our students to be in school did not align with the version they had to be when they were outside of school. Our boys were expected to act differently on the block than they were expected to act in school; being able to change back and forth and adapt to the different expectations was necessary for survival.

We also see this tension manifest in the students' physical interactions. This, I would suggest, is largely a cross-demographic "boy" issue. There is a physicality in boys' learning just as there is in their socialization. Their interaction—their play—is often marked by pseudo-fighting and rough-housing. Whether it is grabbing and pushing and pulling or slap-boxing, this type of physical interaction clearly does not belong in an academic, professional setting; it is, nevertheless, prevalent at our college preparatory school and prevalent in the lives of boys.

For that reason, we must constantly remind ourselves of this internal conflict our students experience moment to moment as members of our school community. What we may view as vestigial elements of antiquated masculine identity, they may view as integral components of their beings. Therefore, we have to consider how to honor the whole of our students while inculcating a broader understanding of what it means to be a man.

What Do We Prioritize—A Safe Environment for Students to Learn or a Safe Environment for Teachers to Teach?

This question should be easy to answer: We are here for students first. But the reality is that it is challenging to be present for students and patient with their transgressions when the language, actions, or expressions of those students become marginalizing and demeaning. If teachers are made to feel unsafe or unvalued because of students' behavior, how can they prioritize serving the very students who may contribute to those feelings? And yet that is what we ask of our teachers—to teach students with patience, compassion, and empathy. Those qualities are integral to teaching, and our school was formed to be a place where students can grow and learn from a faculty that exhibits those qualities. Achieving a cultural pluralism in our school that acknowledges student backgrounds but also holds

---

*A pseudonym is used to protect the confidentiality of the student.

them accountable to the broader community's expectations is a challenging feat. A school community—any community—does not get there without some hurt, some struggles, some frustration, and some disappointment.

In the wake of our assembly, our faculty members prioritized their roles as educators and champions of the students, despite their emotional wounds. They were hurt and frustrated. They felt betrayed. But they also wanted to take the time to recognize why such a large gap existed between the students' interpretations of the assembly experience and their own. Furthermore, they embraced the importance of understanding the difference in experience that existed even between the faculty members. As a team, everyone recognized the value of exploring how so many people were processing this information in so many different ways. So our team remained teachers—with all the honorable values the title suggests—and agreed that the first priority was the need to better understand the students.

We recognized the importance of dispassionately identifying how our students' mindset has taken shape. We discussed and owned the impact of our community's and our nation's history with regard to the justice system and Black men. One of the first communications I received during this period was from a faculty member who, though hurt and deeply offended by students at the assembly, cited clear historical cases of false accusation against Black men and the dire consequences they have had on the Black community. While we did not have to agree with the students or like what they said, we did have to acknowledge that the inputs feeding their opinions and perspectives on these matters might differ from ours.

We agreed that we are not achieving our mission if our students only understand manhood as it is linked to their athletic or sexual prowess—if they do not emerge from the Boys' Latin experience with a clear sense that their manhood is greatest when it embraces vulnerability, respects the strength of femininity, honors the empowerment of women, and empathizes with all members of a community. We want our boys to understand that manhood is about leadership, but it is also about "followership," too. We want them to understand that manhood is about initiative and independence, but it is about brotherhood, too. And we want them to understand that the health of their future relationships—both professional and personal—will rely on their ability to value this broad, powerful, and nuanced definition of their masculinity. That is the only way to truly "prepare [our] boys for college success and beyond."

OUR RESPONSE

Healing needed to happen in our school. But the road to recovery was not, and still is not, clear. The answer, our response, lay somewhere in this dissonance—in the tension between the toughness the world expects of our boys and the refinement it also demands of them. While our growth and healing at Boys' Latin remains ongoing, we did take steps to nurture our own learning as educators as well as the learning of our boys.

We made a decision to facilitate discussion amongst ourselves before addressing these issues with our students. Our first session with faculty was designed to deepen our collective understanding of why what happened at the assembly impacted all of us because it impacted some of us. Moreover, we sought to broaden our understanding of identity, apply the learning to our interactions with colleagues, and identify next steps for personal and professional growth. In doing so, we as a team made the explicit commitment to assume the best, speak our individual truths, seek to understand, accept non-closure, and engage courageously. The session saw us exploring some cutting questions that put pressure on us to reflect. We went on to explore steps the school should take to address issues of concern. Faculty were given opportunities to publicly or privately share ideas with closing writing prompts and writing stems.

This session, led by a local researcher, educator, and specialist on identity and marginalization felt to me, at times, very invasive and confrontational. But that was the point, I guess—to address our unexpressed feelings of sorrow, anger, and confusion. Then again, to others, the meeting did not feel invasive or confrontational enough. We knew this meeting alone would not be sufficient to work through the issues. Many left still frustrated; many left still resentful. Some left with forgiveness or with peace. Some resented that others had been forgiven without having acknowledged any wrongdoing. But we knew we needed to care for ourselves if we had any chance of serving our students, and this was our start.

While our work as a faculty was only beginning, we knew we needed to direct our attention to students and their learning. I connected with educational leaders and community organizations, including Women Organized Against Rape (WOAR), Planned Parenthood, and local universities to solicit expertise and guidance on how to best address issues of gender bias and rape culture with students. We decided to facilitate a program with nearby Temple University and Planned Parenthood that focused on rape culture and consent. We sought to engage students in a discussion about consent and their human responsibility to treat others with respect, reverence, and appreciation. Students were broken into groups, and each group participated in a workshop that presented them with case scenarios designed to illustrate an understanding of consent. These engaging workshops heightened students' awareness. The workshops also evidenced our need for this work, as there was clearly ignorance about the responsibility of men in sexual relationships as it pertains to consent.

An essential preface to these workshops was an opening plenary session designed to build students' capacity to empathize. I explained that, judging from their actions and reactions at the assembly, I was not confident they were opening their minds to information, to facts, and to truths. I chastised them for demonstrating a lack of respect for women who have been victimized and who have spoken out against sexual violence.

However, what was most powerful in this session were the voices of the teachers—of different genders, generations, and races—speaking about their own experiences. They shared very personal accounts and life experiences. Several male teachers talked about the influence and life-saving strength and love of women in their lives. Female faculty, who were already respected in the school for their strength and intellect, shared stories of their own victimization. They helped students understand the mindset of a woman who has been victimized and how we victimize her again when we reject her truth.

As their teachers spoke, students were silent and listened intently. Some were shamed, and some were moved; the hope is that they all learned.

We were taking steps as a faculty and a community. Our workshops with students, though just a beginning, sought to instill an understanding of their responsibility as young men and as members of our community. But we the faculty, the other members of that community, still needed a closer coming together. It was at this time that we reached out to a local leader on relationships to help guide our team toward some common understandings.

She facilitated a session that explored how we could make gender equity an integral component of our work, our professional development, and our learning as a faculty. The aim of her workshop was to help us better understand and counter the micro-aggressions, language, and attitudes that undermine equity. We explored what type of common language students and staff are using that is divisive and how to collectively address it. Ultimately, we talked about how to best be allies for one another, and how to begin recognizing the intersections of our identities. We talked using celebrity culture as our examples. The conversation was informative but very distant from us as individuals and as a group. It felt very safe. Gossip magazines and news stories were the fodder for our exploration of sexism, equity, and identity. It made the session fun, engaging, safe, and comfortable.

We began planning a follow-up session for our back-to-school Professional Development series. This session was designed to explore the concept of intersectionality and to be an interactive consciousness-raising on our intersecting identities. We sought, again, to better understand one another so that collectively we could make sure our students understood these issues as well. Planned for this upcoming session were topics that would challenge our comfort levels and push us to grapple with our preconceived notions and prejudices. Our taskforce developed several scenarios to prompt dialogue. This session, too, was meant to be a starting point for better understanding, for healing, for continued conversations, for more empathy, and for growth.

The next stage of our strategic planning sought direction and feedback from students. Again, we called on an external consultant to ensure that the students would be comfortable giving candid responses. A student focus group made their concerns clear. Their views included typical and valid concerns about school lunches and uniforms. Perhaps more impressive was their call for continued attention to conduct and manners, more emphasis on social and emotional health, and courses addressing health and life skills. Our intent is to continue these critical conversations and embrace the discomfort, recognizing the work as a service to our school community and to our boys.

MY PERSONAL INQUIRY

I value harmony in an organization. In *Now, Discover your Strengths*, Buckingham and Clifton (2001) describe this leadership trait:

> [I] look for areas of agreement. In [my] view there is little to be gained from conflict and friction, so [I] seek to hold them to a minimum. When [I] know that the people around [me] hold differing views, [I] try to find the common ground. [I] try to steer them away from confrontation and toward harmony. (p.101)

The value I place on harmony is perhaps my greatest strength and my greatest weakness. Surely it creates an environment for many that is conducive to growing, learning, and the essential risk-taking I value in our organization. But I know it inhibits me at times as well.

I have known that students use inappropriate language; I have known them to objectify women; I have known that the faculty experiences frustration about these matters. And I have addressed it with individuals—especially students—as matters have arisen. But I should have let the collection of these issues inform my thinking proactively. I should have embraced the disharmony as a learning moment for our entire community long before it reared its head in that assembly. I wish I could say that all the steps we have taken and will take are being done proactively—a result of my foresight, intelligence, and keen awareness sharpened by years of experience. But instead, my response was late, and it was reactive. Prior to the assembly, I attempted to hold conflict and friction to a minimum. I addressed student or teacher infractions in isolation and did not take the time to recognize them as canaries in the mine. I handled these issues individually rather than addressing them holistically, as a school family. I failed our students and our staff in that way. That is the downside of harmony as a leadership value. There can be no growth without sometimes embracing the struggle and discord. I have to learn that aspect of leadership.

Albert Einstein famously noted, "If I only had an hour to solve a problem, I'd spend the first 55 minutes understanding the problem and the last 5 minutes solving the problem." Well, I am no Einstein. But Einstein was no school principal either. I took a considerable amount of time trying to understand this problem, but in doing so, I neglected to communicate promptly with our school stakeholders. I want to believe this came from an Einsteinian place of diligence and care for this serious matter. But I have to acknowledge what may have been an underlying resistance to confessing my uncertainty. Perhaps if I could not have harmony, I wanted to have control, or at least the image of being in control. I think that may have prevented me from communicating as effectively as I should have with faculty through these struggles. My response was quick: I opened my door, listened to stakeholders, and reached out to local experts. I began to plan, but I never communicated that plan until it was in place. And I never took the time to realize how that may have felt to those on the outside. Others had every reason to believe I was simply ignoring this issue. While I was giving the issue much thought and working with a team to address the matter, it was all done behind closed doors. Weeks went by between the assembly and my first official communication to the entire school community. To some, that interim time looked like a tacit acceptance of the students' behavior.

Insecurity got the best of me. My rationale was to come up with a plan and communicate it once it was finalized. But there is a happy medium there that I missed, a space where others are informed and involved in the planning on a broader scale even before—especially before—it is complete. At the very least, this lets stakeholders know their leaders care and understand. It conveys that we are allies. At best, it makes the ultimate plan better.

As a school leader in an all-boys school, fighting the tide of misogyny that can otherwise pervade our school relationships and dynamics is of paramount importance. But for me to believe that my outlooks and perspectives on manhood alone will counter that tide is short-sighted. I have to understand the intersectionality of all our identities in the school. I have to fortify my own understanding of manhood by seeking a stronger understanding of the female experience in our school, the White experience in our school, and the LGBTQIA experience in our school. I have to refrain from making decisions in isolation. Being a Black man is not enough. Creating an ongoing forum where these voices are part of the dialogue that shapes my thinking, influences my leadership, and thus shapes the school experience for our boys is critical.

My leadership will likely remain messy and imperfect. But our learning over the course of these months at Boys' Latin does provide a foundation on which we can continue to build a stronger school culture. We are developing a clearer platform and banner for what masculinity looks like in our school as it pertains to our mission. The intersectionality work we are doing is the basis for this new understanding. Recognizing the interconnected nature of our social constructs and categories as overlapping and interdependent systems of discrimination, disadvantage, privilege, and bias is essential to this work. This, of course, makes the work increasingly challenging, inefficient, and complex. But embracing this nuanced, untidy overarching truth is the way to honor our students and the pieces of ourselves. Teaching our boys about manhood must be couched in an understanding of how manhood connects and intersects with other and all aspects of student identities. So long as we can ensure that part of their identity is Boys' Latin student, we can empower them to be the kind of man we want them to be. And if we do our work right, the man we want them to be is the man they will want to be as well.

REFERENCE

Buckingham, M., & Clifton, D. O. (2001). *Now, discover your strengths.* New York, NY: Simon & Schuster.

CHAPTER 7

"Smart Like a Boy"

The Experiences of Women in an All-Boys Jesuit School

Kristin Ross Cully

Kristin Ross Cully is director of research development and global initiatives with the Jesuit Schools Network of North America. Previously, she served as the principal of Loyola School in New York City. Before that she spent 15 years at Regis High School, an all-boys Jesuit secondary school also in New York City, where she served as the director of guidance and college advisor prior to spending her final 6 years there as assistant principal. Ross Cully has served on the New York Province Secondary Education Advisory Board, and has been a member of the board of trustees at Regis Jesuit High School in Colorado, St. Peter's Preparatory School in New Jersey, and other schools in the northeast region of the United States. She earned a doctorate in educational leadership from the University of Pennsylvania as well as a Master of Education in psychological counseling and a Master of Arts in organizational psychology, both from Teachers College, Columbia University. She has a Bachelor of Science in psychology and education from James Madison University.

I was thrilled to be asked to return for a second round of the interview process at Regis, with my visit to entail a demo lesson to the students on a topic of my choosing. One of the final candidates for a senior counseling spot in a prominent Jesuit high school, I entered the imposing, Ionic-columned landmark building on Manhattan's Upper East Side, and made my way to the third-floor classroom. I do not recall being nervous. That changed the moment I entered: Most of the students looked to be around my age, if not older; several had full beards, and all of them were physically bigger. I had taught boys before, but I had never been the only female in the room. *So, this is what they mean by an all-boys school?* I was 24 years old.

I got the job and spent 15 years working and learning in a Jesuit school community that deeply roots me and has become a part of who I am. As in any professional setting, my experiences in an all-boys school varied widely. At times, I was keenly aware of being the only woman in the room, like when I walked into our quadrangle in the afternoon of a snowstorm and noticed that the crowd of sophomores gathered went instantly silent when they saw me approaching. As the corner of my eye caught the anatomically correct male snowman they were building, I immediately knew why. I suppressed my inner laughter, gave the authoritative look I have perfected in my role—the one that reads *you're more mature than that and I expect better of you*—and down came the snowman without a word said. Or the time when I had to confront a young man about the pornographic Japanese anime he had been caught viewing on one of the school's computers. I am still not sure who was more uncomfortable in that conversation, but I do know I was aware in that moment of my own grappling with the complexities of being a woman working with teenage boys.

Certainly, I have been conscious of being perceived through the lens of gender, for example, when a young man sees me struggling to carry a lot of books and offers to help, or when a door is held open for me, or a rush is made by the boys to get me a chair when there are not enough in a group setting. On a more pragmatic level, I see that both parents and faculty seem to feel comfortable coming to me with concerns. I wonder whether this sense of accessibility is rooted in my approachable demeanor, in my introduction into the community via a counseling role, or in the fact that I am the only woman on the administrative team. While these are not negative experiences, they do remind me that I am a woman in this largely male world.

I chuckled when I moved into my role as assistant principal, the first female administrator in the almost 100-year history of the school, and people asked me if I would now be wearing suits every day to work, as the male administrators before me had done. When I lightheartedly responded that I was more of a dress and skirt kind of girl, I hoped they understood that I intended to approach my new position in a manner that was authentic to who I am as a person and professional, and not try to fit into a prescribed definition of what that role should be.

In an environment where smart and competent young women are not present as peers with our students in classrooms, women on faculty and staff fill a gender void. I am proud that the boys see me as a female leader, a key figure, a decision-maker within a tradition-rich school. By positioning me as a senior school leader, the institution sends a message of support for this vision.

Events at graduation one year gently nudged the gender discussion into the open. I accompanied the president, a Jesuit priest, on the altar to distribute awards. Many of the boys who approached to receive an award gave me a hug. The president, who got a hand shake from the boys, joked with me, "Why aren't I getting a hug?" An apparently simple occurrence, it generated some of our first explicit discussion of gender. We both saw it as a positive and appropriate action by the boys. The hugs felt warm, supportive, and respectful in tone. It felt like a small, positive recognition of difference, innocently expressed, but the door had opened slightly on a much larger question: How does gender function at Regis? As the now senior female leader, how do I lead in such a way as to incorporate this inquiry into a seldom-discussed aspect of our community?

I have always felt respected by faculty and administrative colleagues as well as by students within our community. That is not to say that my experience has been without challenge, especially in my early days, nor have I been immune to my general perception that the boys can be tough on young, female faculty. I recall my first few years in the school feeling very much an outsider to a place where everyone else seemed to know the rules. I felt like I had to work hard to be viewed among the students as competent and knowledgeable, two qualities that are held in high esteem in such an intellectual community. I look back on those early days now and wonder how my gender was at play in my introduction into the community. How might my understanding of who I am as a woman have shaped my perception of these challenges? What potential limitations were there to my understanding of gender in this context?

I decided that I needed to hear from women directly, at least those in fellow Jesuit, all-boys schools. What were other women's experiences in these communities? I offered a roundtable session at a regional colloquium, held every 3 years, of the full faculties, administrations, and staffs of the six Jesuit high schools in our state. The participating women were encouraged to discuss their experiences working in an all-boys Jesuit school. A bit anxious, I asked a few colleagues to lead the session with me, and we developed some talking points to get the discussion underway, mostly focused on the relationship between the female teacher and her students. The well-attended conversation quickly took off, hands raised rapidly around the room, with women eager to share their stories and experiences. Some spoke of the power of female faculty to positively impact students while others told stories of difficulties experienced in their schools between male and female colleagues. For example, several women saw an insidious relationship between the dominating athletic programs of their schools and negative aspects of the culture of gender. To some, a prominent athletic culture allowed a "boys will be boys" attitude within the school. Others shared their sense that being one among a few was not recognized as all that significant within their communities, and given this silence around their gender, they appreciated being asked about their experiences in the session.

I wasn't at all prepared for these stories; they were so foreign to my own experience at Regis. Pleased by the evident interest—so many took the time to thank us personally for opening the conversation—and yet bothered by the extent of the challenges raised, I felt an urgency in understanding what might be going on in the community I served. These wonderings eventually grew into an evolving series of conversations around gender that I have led over the past 7 years.

GROWING A CONVERSATION AROUND GENDER

In all my years as a faculty member, I had never had an explicit conversation about how being a woman might influence my work with the boys. The topic had not been raised in our community. Indeed, the particular experiences of the female faculty members had never before been acknowledged in a formal setting. I sought to change that, because I sensed learning could come from asking questions that had not been asked before. I soon became aware that many of the experiences I had are shared by my female colleagues; many others are not, and some women have faced far more challenges in working with boys than I ever did. In my supervisory role, I needed to understand the challenges faced by all my female colleagues, however they aligned with or differed from my own.

With the encouragement of the colloquium experience behind me, and the support of advisors in my new doctoral program, I gathered a group of female faculty and began a conversation collectively exploring how female faculty members conceptualized their role working in our all-boys Jesuit school. We sought to build a community of inquiry, to create a space to learn together about the roles we shared and the challenges we faced in working with boys.

Sensitive to the fact that this topic was a new one within our tradition-oriented, predominantly male community, I felt it important to move carefully and purposefully as I attempted to get the group off the ground. Prior to sending the initial invitation to the female faculty to join the group, I solicited support for its founding from the president and principal, as well as from our province (or regional) office. While Regis has a true collegial spirit, our culture is steeped in a history of male hierarchy. I needed to build support within that hierarchy for our collective learning effort and for the shift in culture I hoped would result, encouraging talk about gender. I received this backing and sent invitations to the 24 full- and part-time female faculty members; participation was voluntary. We met seven times over the course of the school year, each meeting lasting about an hour. I made it clear to the female faculty in the invitation that all were welcome to attend, and attempted to create a sense of the team as more of a "gathering" and less of a "meeting," with an eye toward encouraging their voluntary participation. I tried to create a space where the women would look forward to attending, and most importantly, would feel comfortable in sharing their thoughts. After the second meeting, I began to receive emails and visits from some of the women, continuing conversations begun in the group setting. Some women described discussions with female colleagues outside of the group meetings, an encouraging sign of a more shared ownership of our inquiry, of a conversation they were eager to have. It was clear there was value in moving forward to think even more deeply about these ideas.

Over the next 2 years, we extended and deepened the modes of our inquiry further, as documented in my dissertation exploring the experiences of women working at Regis (Ross, 2014). Because of the emerging sense of collegiality among the group members, and my strong belief that everyone owns the mission of the school, I expanded the inquiry to invite every woman employed at Regis to participate in the inquiry, including the cafeteria, maintenance, and support staff as well as teachers and counselors. It had become clear in our initial group conversations that every woman in the school, not only those who work directly with the boys, should have a voice in this conversation. The female assistant to our dean of students, for example, deals with hundreds of boys in the various attendance and disciplinary issues that arise in her office. Her job would be categorized as support staff, yet she likely has as many personal interactions with the boys than many classroom teachers, if not more. Her voice, and that of all the other women who play important roles in the school, needed to be a part of this conversation. I was thrilled that 34 of the 37 women in the building voluntarily agreed to participate.

LEARNING FROM THE INQUIRY

One of the great blessings of this inquiry was the privilege of moving beyond my own personal story to hear the stories of my colleagues, and ultimately, getting to share the stories of those who have not been heard before. I recall vividly when one female faculty member shared an experience that stuck out from her first year in the school. She was at her desk with a student in his junior year and they were talking about something from class. The young man said to her, "Ms. X, you are smart like a boy" (Ross, 2014, p. 180). She stopped and responded, "Well that is nice, but, I am smart like a girl . . . girls are smart." The student got embarrassed and she said, "No, I know you meant that comment as a compliment, but it is funny that it came out that way" (p. 180). The teacher shared that she knew that "he was trying to say, Ms. X you fit in here, you are one of us . . . I don't know if they didn't expect me to be smart, or to be able to roll with them, but he said I was smart like a boy!" To me, this anecdote offered insight into the complex experiences of being a woman in a predominately male culture like Regis. It reminded me a great deal of my own sense of being an outsider in my early days. The student apparently wished to convey that she was "one of us," so to speak, and yet he did so by calling attention to her intelligence in a gendered way. What did this reflect about how intelligence, so valued in this community, was seen? Why was the norm of intelligence, for him, a male one? Why is being smart like a boy different in this culture from being smart like a girl, or just being smart? Certainly, these were big, challenging questions but our inquiry had opened a door to this fundamental conversation, one that had not been raised before.

From the earliest point of our initial group meetings, a richness emerged from the shared experiences among the women. Themes of acknowledging gender's influence on relationships, exposing challenges in early years at Regis, and building support among the female faculty were evident. The women were aware of their own gender across the many layers of their work, and they carried this awareness throughout their various roles. They spoke about the challenge of feeling the need to be perceived as serious-minded in their early years in the school, to be viewed as credible when still an unknown member of the community breaking in to the boys' world (Ross, 2014). Were the women, I wondered, working to be perceived as "smart like a boy"? Was this perception of being serious-minded a gendered one? The women enjoyed the support they felt in our inquiry group, in sharing these stories, and in hearing those of their colleagues.

As the inquiry deepened, I learned to describe the experience of being a woman at Regis through a number of different lenses, in an effort to weave some common meaning across so many stories and experiences. The first was an awareness of the physicality of being a woman in a predominantly male setting that seemed to be shared among the women. Across the school, the women were keenly aware of their physical being within their interactions with the boys—from their proximity in the classroom to their sense that modesty in their personal dress was important. The conversations also revealed a sense among the women that the particular space they are in with the boys can affect their experience of gender in the school. The teaching faculty noted that they are not typically aware of their gender when they are in their classrooms. One teacher said:

> When I'm teaching, I think the power structure of the classroom removes gender . . . somebody once told me when I first started teaching like that's your house, when they (the students) walk in it's your house and it's your domain and you call the rules. (Ross, 2014, p. 102)

When asked where the women are most conscious of their gender, the data showed a pattern of responses that involved less structured spaces, such as extracurricular offices, hallways, and department resource centers. It seems as if the space that does not demand content knowledge or expertise leaves a teacher feeling, as one described, like "a woman with a bunch of boys" (p. 102). Once again, it seemed to me, the women can become a part of the boys' world when their competence and expertise are unquestioned. Another participant captured the experience when she said, "I don't think gender is constantly on everyone's mind, but instead it is like background music that now and then becomes obvious" (p. 133).

The women also spoke at length about navigating norms within the school. They understood how their own styles of communication in the classroom may differ from the traditionally debate-oriented styles of communication that permeate the academic culture of Regis, and they can see the tension this may cause. They perceived that the debate-oriented nature of the school reflected the male culture and is different from perhaps more stereotypically "feminine" ways of fostering discussion through collaborative means.

Others felt challenges to authority. "When I think of challenges, I don't think I am directly challenged in the classroom," shared one teacher, "in that I have never experienced a student being outright disrespectful" (p. 112). She continued:

> I think the challenge has come when I have gotten feedback from the students . . . from what I was trying to do, or trying to get across, or who I am as a teacher and my expectations, somehow did not translate. . . . In the course reviews it was noted I was picky and too detailed and not letting them have their opinion. (p. 112)

Another woman shared that in her experience "students ask more frequently for a change of grade or an extension to a female teacher" (p. 152). This insight echoed with my own anecdotal experience, where I often found the students more willing to question the younger female members of our faculty. One participant shared that she had experienced a parent questioning her at a parent–teacher meeting, asking her how long she had worked in the school and where she went to college (p. 152). Her impression was that this was rooted in a questioning of her authority and place in the school. The others in the group seemed to feel that parents, as well as students, will push and challenge new, young female faculty to a greater extent than their more tenured colleagues. (Many in the group said they had not experienced this themselves, but recall it happening with other female colleagues.) It is fair to say that both age and experience were perceived by the women to be at play, as well as the perception of gender.

From some group conversations, an interesting distinction emerged based on age and experience of the women. I remarked that I had heard that women at Regis must be self-confident in order to be successful. The women with fewest years in the school, a group which also included the youngest women, agreed fully with this sentiment. They spoke at length about the need to be confident because of the intellectual caliber of the boys. They viewed self-confidence as an essential trait because of the highly rigorous, scholarly culture.

For more veteran teachers, their emphasis shifted; they noted not self-confidence as essential for success, but self-awareness. One woman, a seasoned department chair with 13 years in the school, said:

> Confidence is there, but I think that's true across genders. I think a guy needs to be just as confident as a woman in the classroom. But I think for women, there's got to be some self-awareness and self-acceptance and sense of self, you know, to allow ourselves to become comfortable not knowing an answer, but knowing we can get it for you the next day. (p. 161)

There is an important distinction there, based on age and experience. How did gendered notions of intelligence intersect with perceptions of age?

Finally, our conversations, formal and informal, uncovered a pervasive set of "grassroots" efforts related to gender. Apparently independently, various women faculty found ways to lean into gender perceptions in their classrooms. The women expressed how this occurs both overtly and behind the scenes: within the crafting of curriculum, by virtue of their visible roles within the community, and in their more socially-minded interactions with the students. One teacher, the longest-serving female faculty member, described:

> [I feel] like I'm contributing some grassroots feminism in my classes, regarding pointing out sexism in the German language, exposing the boys to a form of indirect gender studies, for example, allowing them to discover the cultural construction of male and female roles via our literature. (Ross, 2014, p. 116)

For example, she explains to the boys:

> even in the beginning levels we do not say Fraulein anymore in Germany. Everybody is Frau . . . because it used to be this distinction if you were not married, but now that does not matter anymore. So now it is considered sexist if you say Fraulein. (p. 116)

This teacher believes strongly in her self-initiated role in furthering a feminist perspective within the community:

> I think that for our boys, it's a great advantage to see that they get a representation of women in the school by having teachers and others being women that is not the male-clichéd advertisement of women. So, we're not Barbie dolls. We're very intellectual people who also happen to be women. (p. 128)

As a leader, I was learning a great deal about faculty insights, generated over years. These would have been invisible had we not begun talking publicly, trying to make sense of how gender played out in our school.

Another participant wished to show her students that, as a woman, she is not one-dimensional, that there is more to her life than being their teacher. She was also aware of her interactions with her male colleagues (i.e., how she carries herself in the school) and the messages the boys take from these interactions. She spoke about hearing her students speak dismissively of their female counterparts that they know from home or other schools:

> sometimes they are very dismissive of them in terms of "well, they're not that smart" or "they're not capable of doing these things" and so to me, this need to model that "No, that's not true" . . . and then the active piece of trying to live as this intelligent and confident and interested female." (p. 119)

In a more general way, the presence of the women at Regis serves as a bridge to "the other." As one female colleague noted:

> There's something of a more subtle nature to do, to break down, open up, and air out the tendency to think of women as "Other." It aims to help them experience, come to know and treat women—each of us, individually—as different. (Ross, 2014, p. 124)

This powerful "airing out" or "opening" metaphor speaks directly to the potential for women in the school to alter the contours of the community by the sheer fact of their presence. Yet the women at Regis take it further than this mere presence, as they actively seek to "open up" the predominantly male community by their mindful and intentional efforts related to gender within their work in the school. Another woman explained, "I believe women in Jesuit schools have an incredible opportunity to round out the viewpoints of these young men, to demonstrate the depth of the knowledge and capability we have as women in a predominantly male setting" (p. 125). Another shared that "our role is not to mask our gender to conform, but to show how communities are created as a result of those differences" (p. 125).

WHAT HAPPENED AFTER? LASTING EFFECTS AND THE VALUE OF RAISING THIS INQUIRY

The existence of a deliberate effort to address gender signaled a legitimate learning challenge to the community (Reichert, 2001). This inquiry suggests that the simple act of raising the question prompted important learning for the broader Regis community. This included an enhanced sense of community among women, reinforcing their place as leaders in community conversation. The women were enthusiastic about their collective exploration, discussing previously unstated common experiences with colleagues and articulating them together. "[O]ne of the biggest takeaways for me," shared one woman, "is that the . . . conversations . . . have created a connectivity amongst us that I think will last" (Ross, 2014, p. 187).

One has to wonder: In a Jesuit culture where reflection is valued, why had community reflection not previously extended to gender? Was this due to the small number of women in the community before the past decade or so? Did it require a senior female leader to raise the subject of gender and give it credibility and energy within the community, to authorize this conversation on a public level? Did the limited role of women in the wider Catholic Church have an influence as well?

Beyond Regis: A National Conversation Blooms

As principals of all-boy Jesuit schools around the country heard about our inquiry, some invited me to present to their faculty and staff. Often, these invitations followed a reaction to some type of negative gender-related incident in the community. For example, one invitation came after a student took an upskirting photo of a female faculty member. Another arrived after contentious gender relations within the student life of the school became inflamed and created a media storm. Just as in the colloquium years ago, I have heard a range of experiences from women in different settings, and I have left each presentation feeling energized by opportunities for school communities to grow, more open to previously unstated concerns. Often, I would be asked my insight on how to begin this conversation in their community. With just an introduction to their culture, I could offer only a modest first step: *Start a group, and be open to where the inquiry leads you.*

The Effect of Taking This Inquiry Stance on My Own Leadership

Growing this conversation around gender over the course of several years, inside and outside my school, I have learned the value of leading from a place of personal authenticity, by openly sharing my own experiences with those in my community. Sharing my own personal story served to connect me more fully to the women in various discussions, to the women with whom I lead, and to my own sense of myself as a female professional in a male-dominated network. Within a tradition valuing reflection, we explicitly expanded conversation and connection in areas where we had been largely silent and isolated. I learned the value of exploring previously unnamed issues, of not being afraid to open new conversations, of creating space for learning, of opening myself to those around me, and of embracing uncertainty in my leadership. I learned the complexity of the mix of experiences of these women at Regis. Even there, where most felt supported, with a strong sense of ownership, and within an inclusive school culture, some still felt their place challenged at times. Our community, including me, grew in awareness and in our agency to foster inquiry. Looking back, I now realize that this consciousness-raising was just the beginning. I look forward to continuing to be open to what comes next in exploring the experiences of "smart like a boy" women across various school cultures and communities.

REFERENCES

Reichert, M.C. (2001). Rethinking boys' lives: New ideas for schools. In W. Martino & B. Meyenn (Eds.), *Teaching boys: Issues of masculinity in schools* (pp. 38–52). Buckingham, United Kingdom: Open University Press.

Ross, K. E. (2014). *Smart like a boy: The experiences of women working in an all-boys Jesuit school* (Doctoral dissertation). Retrieved from ProQuest Dissertations & Theses Database. (UMI No. 3622667)

Part III

LEADING SYSTEM-LEVEL INQUIRY

CHAPTER 8

Braking and Entering

A New Chief Financial Officer's Transition into a K–12 Urban School District

David Trautenberg

David Trautenberg is deputy chief of finance and operations of Orleans Parish School Board in New Orleans, Louisiana. He was formerly chief financial officer of the Aurora Public Schools, a large semi-urban and predominantly Latino district in Colorado. There, he focused on helping the district align and optimize financial resources to improve students' outcomes. His career path is unusual; before his school district appointments, Trautenberg spent over 2 decades on Wall Street as an investment strategist and firm vice president. He earned his doctorate and master's degree in education from the University of Pennsylvania, an additional MA from University of Leeds (UK) School of Education, his BA from the University of Pennsylvania, and an MBA from the Stanford Graduate School of Business.

Prior to embarking on a Wall Street career and obtaining an MBA, I was briefly a teacher. Twenty years later, while in the midst of a "mid-life crisis," I heard a provocative talk by Geoffrey Canada, founder of the Harlem Children's Zone, that reignited my interest in K–12 public education. Canada challenged his audience to improve opportunities for kids in urban, resource-challenged schools, and in that way help deal with the country's inequities. His talk encouraged me to consider a career change and position myself for transition into K–12 urban education. I contacted Canada to find out what he thought would be the best way for me to re-enter education. He suggested that I immerse myself in a cohort of educational professionals engaged in a mid-career leadership development program. That recommendation led me to enroll in the executive-style doctoral program at the University of Pennsylvania's Graduate School of Education, and within a year, I accepted a position in the Aurora, Colorado, schools.

I used an "entry planning" method based on an inquiry stance, described below, to anchor me as I ventured into an unfamiliar organizational system (see also Trautenberg, 2016). First, I discuss the relationships, processes, and tools that allowed me to make sense of this unfamiliar and complex system. Second, I examine how, as a non-conventional entrant, I worked to develop the trust and learning necessary to my work of aligning the district's resources with its mission of improving students' outcomes. Then, I consider my leadership role in three areas of responsibility—negotiating the teachers' Master Agreement (contract), supervising Nutrition Services, and teaching Bonds 101 to the Board of Education (BOE) and the Aurora Public Schools (APS) community. In considering these examples, I try to capture the complexity associated with transitioning into K–12 education, the need to brake against the knee-jerk tendency to take immediate action without prior sustained inquiry-based learning, and the possibilities for transformational change that can result from introducing fresh perspectives into a system.

GETTING THE JOB

I received an unprompted email from Aurora Public Schools' superintendent alerting me to the district's posting for a new chief financial officer (CFO). To prepare for my interview, I reviewed the district's website, including the district's budget and its audited comprehensive annual financial report, the most recent preliminary offering statement, and a Colorado School Finance Project report.

I paid particular attention to the CFO's job description to determine how the district viewed the role of CFO. Was he/she merely to comply with reporting mandates and maintain the status quo? Or would this person be able to foster cultural and operational change within the bounds of the division? Would the CFO be encouraged to partner with the superintendent in envisioning and driving strategic transformation throughout the system?

During this phase, I learned that APS had cycled through four CFOs in 5 years and that the CFO was historically viewed as a compliance manager who ensured that financial documents were accurately prepared and filed on a timely basis. In contrast, I hoped to become a more strategic education CFO, one who was intimately involved in the district's strategic and capital-allocation decisions, particularly around instruction, and teacher recruitment and retention.

To my amazement, I was offered the position, and I quickly agreed to an October start date. As a novice CFO, I was aware that I faced a challenge in entering a resource- and performance-challenged K–12 urban school district serving 41,000 students, one with a long history of below-standard student achievement.

ASSUMING THE POSITION

As a new and unlikely senior administrator, I had to figure out *how* to enter a large, complex urban K–12 school district, something for which my private-sector experience had not prepared me. I was well aware that I would need to learn the federal, state, and district policies, regulations, and procedures that defined, encouraged, and also impeded resource management. Further, I would need to assess the capacity of the district to carry out its mission.

Having no experience working in the public sector, I realize (in retrospect) that I came with a mindset and approach not altogether suited for this environment. I soon learned that I needed to adopt what I would later recognize as an "an inquiring stance."

During this predictably confusing period of entering, I needed to learn and interpret unfamiliar organizational dynamics while reflexively assessing the environmental impact of my own entry so that I could properly identify areas ripe for change. I recognized that I needed to convey a professional and personal commitment to becoming "local"—by acquiring and accumulating the local knowledge that can only accrue to an individual who commits to becoming, if not a native, then at least a permanent resident of the community. Moreover, I needed to signal to the educational ecosystem that I intended to combine my prior knowledge from Wall Street with an acquired perspective of the educational milieu in which I sought to lead. To address these issues and counteract the reflex to engage in immediate action, I chose to slow down my interaction with the APS ecosystem by applying the brakes of entry planning.

SEEKING COUNSEL ON ENTRY

On the advice of my doctoral program advisor, I decided to email Barry Jentz, one of the authors of *The EntryPlan Approach* (Jentz & Wofford, 2008) and numerous articles related to educational leadership entry. Thus began our collaborative relationship. In Jentz's model, an entry plan begins with a draft of what the new entrant hopes to learn about the organization, its personnel, and its clients during the first several months on the job. The preliminary plan lays out a rationale, process, timelines, and prospective participants; is shared with a few key individuals to get feedback; and is then revised. Before conducting interviews, the questions are shared with participants, and as the data-collecting process proceedes, the emerging observations are shared with participants to ensure transparency and validate findings. Ideally, this inquiry process has the added benefit of creating relational trust for the new leader.

As a critical friend, Jentz agreed to review and comment on the draft of my entry plan. I then presented the revised version to the superintendent for input. Through this document, I wanted to convey the learning activities I would be pursuing while simultaneously fulfilling my stated job responsibilities. The superintendent's response noted the importance of keeping up with what Jentz called "the regular job" while also conducting my interviews and observations.

As opposed to the commonly held notion that new leaders should "hit the ground running" and thus make an immediate impact, entry planning embraces the rationale of "hitting the ground learning" in one's new organizational environment (Jentz & Wofford, 2008, p. 10). My assumption was that individuals who are deliberate in trying to understand an organization's code—the procedures, norms, rules, and forms, as well as the languages, beliefs, and practices an organization relies on to socialize new recruits—may be more successful at introducing themselves into the organizational environment. That is, by being deliberate, the new entrant can slow down his or her rate of absorption by the existing system. My hope was that a thoughtful entry process would provide an iterative draft-test-and-revise cycle of interactions, increasing the likelihood that in my CFO role I would be able to improve the quality of problem posing and defining, and related decisionmaking regarding organizational performance. More importantly, however, this was my approach to taking an inquiry stance as a leader: to use the systematic approach of entry planning to learn from my new context and from others, and to build community.

Having adopted this inquiry process as a way to learn the organization, I developed a set of questions for each employee category (Superintendent's Leadership Team, Divisional, Supportive) and conducted my interview sessions in a conversational format intended to engender trust and transparency. Before the interviews, I made my entry plan public and distributed it to those I planned to interview, underlining the confidential nature of the process. As the interviews progressed, they helped me learn about the relationships, processes, and tools necessary to align and optimize resources at the district level so as to improve student outcomes.

I soon realized that I had entered an organization with a well-established, top-down reporting structure. I was struck by the stark hierarchical nature of its organizational chart, and the fact that students, parents, and the larger community were not included. I wondered if APS's leadership realized how an organizational chart expressed its relational stance with its community, and I determined to develop an understanding of the demographic and geographic context of the system I was entering.

Within APS, the CFO's job description defined my sphere of responsibilities and gave insight as to how the superintendent viewed the CFO position. It focused on the preparation and administration of budgetary and financial matters, and the business functions of accounting, payroll, budgeting, accounts payable, nutrition services, purchasing, warehousing, printing, and grants. Only 10% of the CFO's time was allocated to providing strategic leadership, positioning the CFO as a responder rather than initiator.

During my job interview process, I had become aware of the depth and breadth of the APS controller's experience. In her 33 years of service, she had held every accounting position, acquiring extensive knowledge of our payroll and budgeting IT systems. She was combat-tested, having helped the district manage through the Great Recession and the aftermath of the Aurora Theater shooting. In the interval between job acceptance and start date, I had a series of meetings with her. After each meeting, she provided me with historical financial documents, which included the district's Chart of Accounts, budget models, outside consulting reports related to the division's operational efficiency, and the State's Handbook of Laws. During our conversations, she gave me her perspective on the division's challenges, the departments needing capacity building, technology needs, and the superintendent's expectations. We discussed the difference between the private sector, where people were motivated by profit, and K–12 education, where people were motivated to contribute to and be in service of the collective good. We reviewed some of the office rituals related to meetings, birthdays, and behaviors, and constructed our own confidential rules of engagement, establishing that what we said in our private meetings was not to be shared with others. She accepted the role of master teacher, and I accepted the role of engaged learner. Her assistance and guidance were instrumental in my entry.

My intentions were to generate relational trust (see Bryk, Sebring, Allensworth, Luppescu, & Easton, 2010) with this district veteran, fine-tune my entry plan's interview questions, and confirm whom I needed to meet. I knew that she was critical to my onboarding, providing me with the mentoring, constructive criticism, and training that were essential to my survival.

Because my role as defined in my job description required me to interact with the district's Board of Education on a weekly basis, I included board members in my entry plan. An elected body, the board consisted of seven individuals whose role was to make policy decisions and delegate responsibility for carrying them out to the superintendent and his leadership team. Two of the BOE members were male, one Black and one White. The one White male board member had previously worked for APS, reporting to the chief accountability and research officer. He now worked for the Colorado Department of Education as its accountability and research manager. Of the five female members, four were White (one Hispanic/non-Spanish-speaking) and one was Filipino. Three out of the seven elected members held doctoral degrees. According to the deputy superintendent, each board member had run unopposed in the previous election. The superintendent was the only district employee who directly reported to the board.

In tandem with our chief academic officer (and many times separately), I was required by the superintendent to meet separately with a BOE member each week. During these meetings, I developed formal and informal patterns of communication, worked to build trust, and tutored each board member in school finance by deconstructing the complexities related to state- and district-wide educational funding. This included discussing more esoteric asset-based financing to accelerate the replacement of our transportation fleet (the oldest in the state), as well as preparing each board member for a crucial general-obligation bond financing central to the district's strategic capital-improvement plan.

THREE ILLUSTRATIONS OF MY EVOLVING ROLE

Entry planning was essential in helping me identify the people, information, relationships, processes, and tools I needed to do my job; and to make sense of this complex system. Through my entry-plan conversations, I acquired a deeper understanding of the structures, codes, routines, norms, and behaviors that defined APS's culture. Respondents steered me to historical documents, artifacts, and outside relational networks. These documents seemed to coalesce around three main categories: relational structures and formal codes/processes/procedures; environmental conditions that sub-organized into regulatory/statutory, political, economic and social; and technology. As new questions emerged related to my data collection, I continued to leverage relationship networks to help me find other necessary materials relevant to my areas of responsibility and to understand how other districts' CFOs approached and addressed challenges I sought to act upon. The three cases which follow provide illustrations of the benefits of entry planning—teacher contract negotiations, nutrition services management, and bond issuance.

The Teacher Contract

I was not informed of my role regarding the teachers' Master Agreement negotiations until just before the proceedings began, nor included in prior strategy meetings. Because many of the district's negotiating positions were influenced by the complex interactions of the state's legislative actions, I realized I needed to get up to speed quickly to become an effective contributing member to the BOE's negotiations team.

To accelerate my learning process, I searched for other knowledgeable district employees who, like the controller, were willing to help me get up to speed. I accepted my position as a "rookie" on a team composed of experienced members—both the BOE and the Aurora Education Association's negotiations team—with the chief personnel officer and the deputy superintendent in particular actively scaffolding my learning. I found that these individuals, many of whom were previously teachers and principals, were unhesitatingly generous with their time and insights. They shared their experiences as they instructed me in the finer points of the teacher contract. In the process, I recognized that my vulnerability in being a new entrant could be used as an asset.

As I learned, teacher contract negotiating is a highly complex process because it impacts individuals' workplace conditions and future compensation. Negotiations have a shape, ebb, and flow that involve separate, but intertwining, complex systems. These oscillations are directly influenced by the state legislature's budgetary proceedings. Consequently, the actors in these negotiations initially focus on "softer" issues such as teacher evaluations, contact and planning time, middle school staffing ratios, and grievance procedures, and only later move on to the "hard" issues of compensation and benefits. Because most of these early issues concerned either instruction or evaluation, areas not in the CFO's direct purview, I had the luxury of observing interactions led by the experienced Human Resources Chief. This allowed me to work through my own trepidation about not wanting to make a major gaffe if called upon to estimate costs of new initiatives, while not yet understanding the district's educational jargon. That required making sense of the process; uncovering the relationships and tools necessary to successfully and responsibly execute the work; and cultivating mutual trust, safety, and respect among parties dependent on one another to succeed.

Entry planning helped me uncover a treasure trove of useful historical data to aid in this process. Prior years' negotiations "binders," climate surveys, and anecdotes accelerated my onboarding process. The parties to the negotiations—other district CFOs, educational reporters, policy reformers, think-tank professionals, legislators, and lobbyists—breathed life and new understanding into those documents, providing a nuanced contextual understanding of the proceedings.

I learned the importance of monitoring legislative activity and interpreting its significance to the board and the educational community. And I became clearer about how to analyze and explain the implications of prospective contract terms to the negotiating team and the Board of Education. Most important, my inquiry stance and my genuine desire to be transparent to the district's local teachers' union representatives engendered continuing good will with teachers and other school leadership members who came to observe our negotiations, which by state law are public. The outcome was satisfactory to all parties—a manageable salary increase matched by significant concessions from the teachers.

Nutrition Services

As supervisor of the Nutrition Services division, I relied on my formal MBA training and private market experience to understand it as a business enterprise, applying a Wall Street analyst's perspective. Nutrition Services was viewed by the district as a self-supporting "business"—an enterprise that was in my private sector wheelhouse. Once I understood the department's unique patois, I brought an analytical and managerial confidence to this milieu.

But the school cafeteria was my real classroom. I went there first to observe and then to participate in its daily operations. By mapping the delivery of inventory from the warehouse into the kitchens' refrigerators and freezers, I was able to get an operational feel for the business. I rolled up my sleeves and served student meals with the kitchen staff, a group of employees who generally feel invisible to central office leadership. I ate food prepared in our kitchens. I breakfasted and lunched with employees and students, learning from their conversations. I led by just showing up, being genuine in my inquiries, and making sure staff and students had easy access to me. I served food, tied shoes, helped wipe noses, and made sure I followed up on all inquiries.

Before I entered APS, I had been advised by a seasoned urban K–12 CFO to transfer Nutrition Services to another division because it was a low-status, operational department. But as I came to understand, food service staff were important and valuable employees. They interacted with our kids, no matter what color or ability, in non-classroom settings. I learned how they perceived the quality of schooling in APS, the importance of the District's health benefits plans to their families, and how their school's leadership was doing. Because most of these employees lived in our district, I also got a community view as well.

Through my entry planning activities, I came to regard our kitchen staff as efficient and effective allocators and managers of our resources (something I discovered because I was relegated to serving dessert until I learned how to be faster in portioning out food). Their collective commitment to student well-being helped us become the first urban district in the state to qualify for the USDA's Community Eligibility Program. Not only did this increase our federal lunch reimbursements, it also removed the stigma typically borne by students who received free meals.

Bonds 101

A school district's CFO is formally responsible for advising the superintendent and BOE regarding its school-financing strategy and optimal debt composition, including the types of financing instruments and amounts. In addition to the district's ability to pay, investors look to the quality and stability of its management team. A seasoned CFO is well informed about the district's short- and long-term funding needs, and cognizant of taxpayers' and investors' concerns related to debt amounts, types of debt maturity structures, and the district's ability to meet repayment obligations. During the bond election process and accompanying financial roadshow (when top officers engage the community and investors), the CFO is seen as the point person with credit rating agencies, investment bankers, fiduciary advisors, and potential investors.

I was in my wheelhouse in teaching Bonds 101 to the board and APS community. I knew that the district's preliminary bond offering statements were chock full of financial and descriptive information. In reviewing them, I zeroed in on several topics, shifting my vantage points between the CFO-as-issuer and the individual-as-investor. The most useful sections of the statements were the Introduction, District, District Financial Information, Debt and Other Financial Obligations, and Miscellaneous. These provided an immediate snapshot of the district, including its underlying property values and tax base, its governance structure, enrollment and growth trends, types of charter schools, facilities' conditions, and financial information (i.e., state funding, total program funding, historical uses of general funds, budgeting process, labor relations, state limits on taxing and spending, and retirement and pension concerns). Altogether, these details represented the ingredient list for what a sophisticated investor would want to know before purchasing the district's bonds.

I reached out to our investment bankers, municipal advisor, bond counsel, and outside accountants who were only too willing to give me tutorials on the nuances of school district' funding, issuance constraints, ballot language and timetables, and competitive market forces. This helped me produce a primer and a more advanced presentation on the district's financing challenges and considerations, which opened the way for ongoing dialogue with individual board members. The board quickly recognized my expertise in this area and once I established trust, always acting in a transparent manner, I was able to move financial initiatives forward with alacrity. Not all C-suite leaders achieved this level of trust and collaboration with the board.

As part of my preparation for teaching Bonds 101 to the superintendent and the board, I also reviewed the statutory requirements related to bond issuance and assessed property values. I anticipated the possible need for a ballot initiative to change debt limits from 20% of assessed value to 6% of market value of the residential and commercial property within the district. I next assessed the environmental input. This included regulatory, political, economic, and social factors that defined, encouraged, or impacted the district's operational or educational funding. I kept a watchful eye on the teachers' contract negotiations and legislative bills related to schools.

For strategic reasons I wanted us to be ahead of other school districts and other municipal entities that would also be requesting services and advice from investment bankers. I knew that we needed our bankers' attention and modeling resources to compensate for our division's dearth of analytical capacity, and their tutoring regarding the intricacies of Colorado's laws regarding municipal financing. Recognizing that their services would be in high demand, especially during the summer when school districts and other municipal entities would be considering the mechanics of ballot language and financing structures, we negotiated commitments with these professionals.

Working collaboratively with our outside finance professionals, I made certain that the board knew that I did not have all the answers, but that I knew how to ask questions that would leverage third-party resources to get the data and market intelligence we needed to make well-informed decisions. Through this communal learning approach, I gained the board's trust and confidence, particularly that of the board's president and treasurer, who appreciated the transparency, meticulousness, and passion I brought to financial considerations.

The BOE could then decide on the scope and scale of projects and authorize the district to proceed with a bond election. Meanwhile, I worked with our investment bankers and advisors to determine financial structures that would provide us the required proceeds at the least cost, and prepared to support the superintendent during community engagement and investors' roadshows. The result: Aurora voters approved the $330,000,000 bond issue by a 57% to 43% margin, providing multiple-year funding for a number of essential capital projects.

REFLECTIONS

As a new CFO transitioning into a K–12 urban school district, I saw myself as a positive deviant who through inquiry could generate new thinking among other administrators. My hope was to develop innovative approaches that might improve and make more transparent our district's use of limited financial resources towards its mission of improving our students' outcomes. Prior to entering this K–12 urban school district, I had been immersed in the culture of Wall Street, where I was expected by colleagues and clients to respond rapidly to changing market conditions.

After joining APS, I had to recalibrate my behavior, especially my inclination to take on big challenges and, after developing an action plan, drive change. At APS, I found myself frustrated by my inability to sync with administrative colleagues whose career paths had been shaped by their experiences in education, social work, or law, and who were by profession, and perhaps by nature, more circumspect as a result. I bristled at being told to "hit singles" when I believed bolder action could result in bigger and more impactful outcomes. I had to learn how to be conciliatory in meetings where agendas could not be pushed because addressing them would increase tensions. Insulated from the traditional marketplace where other actors can capitalize on a competitor's misuse or misalignment of resources, I witnessed the continuation and toleration of programs and policies that simply failed to advance the district's educational mission.

The most difficult part of my transition was navigating a district culture that valued consensus building over direct and challenging discourse. As a new entrant transitioning from Wall Street, I came with a form of social intelligence, but it was based on execution, not consensus building. In my prior working world, my focus was to develop relationships that would lead to transactions. In my new K–12 urban environment, I found that my private-sector tenacity, which included a comfort with tension and conflict, was misconstrued as driving my own agenda at the expense of not taking the time to consider other people's views. Unlike Wall Street where I challenged people's statements and behaviors, and they in turn defended their positions in a mutual learning process, I found such a mode of discourse uncomfortable for my APS colleagues. I gradually learned that the phrases "We need to move on," "We will need to discuss this at another time," and the more direct "I need you to stop" were understandable responses to my hard-charging behavior and a cultural aversion to real-time critical discourse.

Although I had been hired to be an irritant, I learned that my superintendent had his own notions of the limits and degree of irritation. Nevertheless, I found that the more I assessed and reflected on my own behavior, the more adroit I became in understanding this human aspect of APS's complex system. By engaging in systematic inquiry into the system and myself, I learned how to interpret a landscape where individuals valued and tolerated consensus building over individual action, where the networking dynamics were driven by individuals who worked hard at developing high levels of emotional intelligence and empathy—unlike the private sector's profit-making or cost-effectiveness imperatives. I realized I had entered a world that was the cultural antithesis of Wall Street's highly competitive, transaction-based, pay-for-performance ethos.

When relational tensions became too great or unresolved, I enlisted leadership coaches—one to make sense of the organization and another to read the relational landscape—to help me become more adept at vantage-point shifting and assessing emotional responses, both mine and colleagues'. Without these critical friends, I could not have survived the knowledge swirl—collecting, analyzing, and trying to understand the interactive dynamics.

As an example, although I had considered restructuring Nutrition Services prior to entry and transferring it to the chief operations officer, I learned during my interviews that a very capable manager led this department. In many respects, Nutrition Services was a model operation, producing fresh meals from scratch that were valued by both students and the larger community. I came to see the cafeteria and its kitchens as a location where I could gain direct insights and feedback from staff who worked and lived in our district. My responsibility for Nutrition Services made it possible for me to be in the schools and to be visible to site leaders. I regularly donned my serving jacket and chef's hat and ventured into our bakery and kitchens. In this way, I tried to earn the respect of the larger school community, and to see the tangible results of connecting financial and in-kind resources to school sites.

Moreover, I found that conducting meetings in my office did not engender the trust and learning necessary to align APS's resources. I discovered that by getting into our cafeterias and our kitchens I garnered student, teacher, administrator, and staff goodwill—not because I showed up, but because I showed up caring, listening, and attending. By walking around schools and volunteering in classrooms, I developed a level of trust and credibility with school administrators. In retrospect, had I entered APS with a "hit the ground running" mindset and transferred Nutrition Services to another division, I surely would have missed these learning opportunities.

I credit *The EntryPlan Approach* (Jentz & Wofford, 2008) for surviving the entry and transition into APS, allowing me to become a contributing member of the district's leadership team. Hitting the ground learning, I was able to identify my direct reports' strengths and weaknesses, and I built a team that improved the district's ability to manage uncertainty and get the things done. In retrospect, I realize that in some ways my entry plan was too ambitious. I could not complete all of my entry planning interviews and data analysis while also performing my daily work routine in my first 90 days. In hindsight, I should have focused my entry plan on uncovering the top three departmental challenges within Finance. Organizationally, we were prone to wasting resources or performing poorly by spreading ourselves too thin.

My shadow had entered the district before I did. Once the superintendent announced my hire, informants used the Internet to garner information about me. My persona was both tarnished and enhanced by my Wall Street experience. Employees harbored fear (of ruthless restructuring) and hope (finally a strong "voice" at the cabinet level) of my arrival. I had not anticipated the cultural dissonance between the private sector, where conflict is viewed as a catalyst for action, and the public sector, where harmony and consensus are more valued.

To my knowledge, little has been written regarding school-district CFO entry. In my view, the education CFO should aspire to the same strategic role as his or her private-sector counterpart: a strategic partner who is involved in all aspects of a district's operations—particularly expenditures on human capital (which generally account for 85% of general fund expenditures)—and tasked with focusing relentlessly on how resources are being used. That would require superintendents (and human resource officers) to shift their own stances, to recruit or develop exceptional candidates who can help transform the traditional role of the K–12 CFO from budgetary administrator to strategic partner. Of course, that would also require that school boards, as the fiscal authorizing entity, and the superintendent, in the role of CEO, consider the CFO as a co-creator of corporate (instructional, operational, and administrative) strategy, allocator of capital to achieve these strategic initiatives, overseer of operations, and partner in external relations to the larger community.

REFERENCES

Bryk, A. S., Sebring, P. B., Allensworth, E., Luppescu, S., & Easton, J. Q. (2010). *Organizing schools for improvement: Lessons from Chicago*. Chicago, IL: University of Chicago.

Jentz, B., & Wofford, J. (2008). *The EntryPlan approach: How to begin a leadership position successfully*. Boston, MA: Leadership and Learning, Inc.

Trautenberg, D. H. (2016). *Braking and entering: A new CFO's transition into a K–12 urban school district* (Doctoral dissertation). Retrieved from ProQuest Dissertations and Theses Database. (Order No. 10125796).

CHAPTER 9

Using Inquiry to Drive System Change

Amy Maisterra

Amy Maisterra currently serves in the District of Columbia's Office of the State Superintendent of Education (OSSE) as assistant superintendent of elementary, secondary, and specialized education. She joined OSSE to contribute to education reforms underway in the District of Columbia and has held several positions within the agency. Previously she had been an administrator in the School District of Philadelphia's Division of Student Services, where she was responsible for implementing court-mandated special education program improvement. She received her doctorate in educational leadership from the University of Pennsylvania, a master's degree from the Smith College School for Social Work, and her bachelor's from the University of Pennsylvania.

The email arrived during my second year as assistant superintendent of special education at the Office of the State Superintendent of Education (OSSE), a relatively new agency in the District of Columbia. I had joined OSSE excited about helping to fix what many saw as a broken system and compelled by the idea of creating an effective agency unencumbered by entrenched practices. In the email, a school asked for guidance on an urgent and complicated special education issue. Over several weeks, the request had traveled across many desks, with well-meaning staff passing it along to others who they thought could better answer the question. Unfortunately, no one had answered the question and the sender had been left hanging. Was this an anomaly or was it a symptom of a larger problem?

Prior to the creation of OSSE, the District of Columbia Public Schools (DCPS), the city's one traditional school system, served as both state education agency (SEA) and local education agency (LEA). Under this structure, DCPS was responsible for holding itself accountable, reporting on its performance to the U.S. Department of Education (USED), and supporting the city's growing and diverse public charter school sector.

In addition to DCPS, DC has roughly 65 public charter LEAs that vary greatly in size, with some serving several schools and others serving just one. To help manage the unique complexity of public schooling in the District, OSSE was created to monitor and provide support to DCPS and the public charter school LEAs. However, clearly identifying this new agency's role was more complicated than anyone had expected, and OSSE's struggle to find its footing was exacerbated by the frequent turnover of middle and upper management. In spite of this, OSSE made significant strides—distributing funds in a timelier manner, building data systems to capture key student information, and providing guidance to LEAs regarding legal requirements and good practice.

My division was charged with overseeing special education. Beginning in the 1990s, DC was sanctioned by both USED and the federal court for its failure to meet obligations set forth in federal law related to serving students with disabilities. USED had placed special conditions on the city's federal special education grant, and the District had been found liable in multiple class action lawsuits related to special education. Our team was charged with turning around the city's performance in this area by developing data systems, monitoring practices, providing training, and creating strong policies. In order to support and maintain such reform, my team of six directors and I needed to ensure that we and our staff worked effectively across these practice areas.

In the email scenario described above, I saw evidence that we might not have gotten it right. I shared with my directors my concerns about our lack of response to an urgent email. They agreed it was problematic, but some noted that it was not surprising given the team's many meetings, priorities, and deadlines. This is the story of my effort to improve ways of thinking and operating, to ensure we were serving those who relied on our support and services well. It is also a story about how uncomfortable, messy, disappointing, and challenging leadership can be.

DISRUPTING THE STATUS QUO

In my view, meaningful change begins with questioning and challenging people on their beliefs. Our charge was to ensure that schools delivered special education services in accordance with the law: specifically, monitoring schools for compliance, providing training to schools on best practice, overseeing funding, and managing special education data systems. Doing so efficiently and effectively with limited resources demanded creativity. At the same time, if people felt stretched thin, introducing new practices could feel burdensome.

During our first meeting, directors expressed differing views on how inquiries should be handled, and more generally on what it meant to be an expert. The meeting was illuminating for me because leaders had different perspectives on how staff should operate in situations of uncertainty. Some felt that staff too readily went "outside their lane" of expertise, posing a risk for the agency. Others were more concerned that staff passed things along too quickly without taking ownership, and too narrowly defined their roles. There was also concern that employees did not feel comfortable asking for assistance when they lacked knowledge, and it became apparent that views differed on whether gaps in knowledge were fundamentally acceptable. This discussion indicated that we were facing both technical and adaptive challenges (Heifetz, Grashow, and Linsky, 2009) as a team. We had a technical challenge related to the quality and timeliness of our responses to LEAs, but we also had differing views about how staff should go about their work.

In response, I brought the group together again to share a proposal, the LEA Support Model. The model would create internal teams comprised of staff from each unit. Each team would be responsible for supporting a specific group of LEAs, such that each LEA would have dedicated staff assigned to it and only one place to go to receive help. To serve in this role, staff would be responsible for learning about their assigned LEAs: their goals, the unique context in which they operated, and their specific challenges. This "one stop shop" support model would allow for LEAs to consult with an interdisciplinary team who could leverage their knowledge of the LEA and available resources in our office to best problem-solve.

The power of this approach became clear to me while working in behavioral health, where it was common for clinicians to participate in "case clinics." Clinicians who felt stuck would present their challenges to a group of peers from psychiatry, psychology, and clinical social work. The group would provide a source of fresh perspectives and possible new strategies for the clinician to consider. While presenters typically started the conversation thinking that the problem was intractable, they would leave the consultation with new insights and renewed hope. A similar process of inquiry was being used in the education field, through tuning protocols initially developed by Brown University's Coalition of Essential Schools and later refined by Blythe, Allen, and Powell (1999). Cochran-Smith and Lytle (2009) refer to a process of inquiry as "a critical habit of mind, a dynamic and fluid way of knowing and being in the world of educational practice that carries across professional careers and educational settings" (p. 120). Perhaps an inquiry-based problem-solving approach would help my team make time for, seek, and solve complex and urgent problems for schools.

LAUNCHING THE MODEL

In sharing my proposal with my team, I acknowledged that I was asking them to take a leap of faith. Many had expressed that they already felt overburdened, and change would demand a significant investment of time and energy when the outcome was unknown. While initially there was some resistance to change, in the end the team was enthusiastic, and we moved forward with their questions on how we would operationalize the model.

The first question focused on prioritization: Specifically, what would implementation of this approach mean in terms of demands on people's time, and where should it rank on the list of existing priorities? What projects could be postponed while we carved out the time needed to do this well? These questions created a dilemma for me: The benefits of this approach were well documented in other settings, yet how many resources should I allocate when the impact of the model was uncertain in this context? Delaying existing projects also introduced risk.

The second question related to the division's readiness for the model—the group was not sure that all staff could shift to this approach. For some staff it would be an easy, exciting shift; others would need extensive guidance and support. This raised an interesting set of considerations. I believed that staff had much more capacity than was recognized, though perhaps I was naïve. Could we create enough checks and balances in the model to guard against performance gaps, and more fundamentally, did we have the right people to do this work (Collins, 2001)?

These questions could not be answered with certainty and there remained some hesitancy within the group. I wondered how much weight should be given to the reservations expressed by the team. For the new approach to be successful, it was clear that I needed my leadership team on board. Spillane, Halverson, & Diamond (2004) speak to leadership as a function of interactions between leaders, followers, and the general environment. It would be everyone's day-to-day choices, interactions, and attitudes that would determine our outcome. At the same time, I remained resolute that the current situation was so problematic that we needed significant improvement, and there was strong evidence that the proposed solution would help achieve this goal. Understanding that I had varying levels of buy-in across my team, I felt that the risk of making a decision to move forward was warranted.

In further discussions with the team, I acknowledged that their questions were important, and that I did not yet have all the answers. I also shared my reasoning for moving ahead and committed to evaluating the effectiveness of the approach and changing course as needed. After this discussion, the team confirmed their willingness to move forward with implementation, and we began planning next steps.

LEARNING TO LISTEN

We launched the LEA support model before the beginning of the next school year. The idea was to support LEAs in two ways: (1) the use of an online web-based application, through which LEAs could submit questions and get a timely, accurate response from their assigned team; and (2) live support via telephone and in-person meetings for more complex problem-solving. LEAs could choose how they would use both mechanisms as they saw fit.

We decided to focus on the online tool first, with the goal of addressing questions about data, policy, and practice. We developed a protocol by categorizing typical questions from LEAs and assigning levels of urgency and associated resolution paths. For example, a question relating to student health or safety would be considered emergent and require an immediate response, whereas complex policy or operational questions would be allotted more turnaround time.

To launch this component of the model, we expanded a tool that was already in use with LEAs to address special education data challenges. Because LEAs had been using the tool and we had evidence that it was effective, it made sense to leverage it for this purpose. All staff were invited to conversations related to the tool's design and the response protocol, and the team was fully engaged. Interestingly, while these conversations were intended to be about the tool, they served a critical secondary purpose of allowing staff to learn about each other's work and their views on how our division should serve LEAs. The conversations were exciting and illuminating. However, as the launch of the expanded online tool grew close, several of my directors raised concerns.

First, the design initially had every inquiry funneled through leaders who had significant responsibilities outside of this project. Some were understandably concerned that reviewing all questions and ensuring timely responses could be a full-time job. They asked that I instead assign dedicated staff who could serve as front-line responders to monitor the flow of inquiries, address minor technical issues, and engage the teams as needed on more complex issues. Upon reflection, this made sense to me. Having high-level resources manage the flow of inquiries was not the best use of their time. I decided to create a separate team that would review and distribute all incoming inquiries.

Second, because the new model made it more convenient to contact our division, some leaders expressed concern that we would receive, and be unable to address, inquiries outside of our area of expertise. In my view, this concern could be addressed through clearly communicating the purpose and scope of the protocol.

Third, some raised further concerns about the readiness of staff to work directly with LEAs (the second component of the model). They felt that more time was needed to prepare staff before the "switch was flipped." Their view was that the online tool should be the focus for the first year, while we worked to prepare staff for deeper engagement across disciplines, allowing gaps in knowledge to be identified and remedied. I continued to question whether the capacity of the staff was being underestimated; however, I also realized that the leaders, who worked directly with our staff, likely knew more than I did. I agreed to the request to move forward with the online tool in the first year and postpone the launch of direct consultations with LEAs until year 2. I asked the team to hold monthly meetings to help staff learn about their responsibilities, become familiar with specific LEAs, and develop their expertise.

Initially, I was concerned that these adjustments would limit the initiative's impact. If I had been more persuasive, or spent more time framing out the contours of the plan, would people be more comfortable with moving forward with all aspects of the model? While it is possible that the answer was yes, it ultimately did not matter. My team had trusted me enough to launch something difficult. Insisting that we follow the original plan after this feedback would have risked losing my strongest leaders, those who were not afraid to question me or push back. It was important to me that I retain a steady flow of creative ideas that might contradict—but be an improvement on—my initial thoughts and plans. In addition, had we launched the consultative work with LEAs prematurely, we would have risked providing misinformation to our schools and damaging the relationships we were trying to strengthen.

Implementing the new model helped us communicate important messages to our staff about our core work and gave them a new framework for understanding their role. They were invited to think about, discuss, and shape how we could do our work differently. We also made significant changes to how we used our online tool to better help LEAs. One of the most exciting outcomes was our ability to track our response times and regularly share them with our LEAs. This change helped us measure our effectiveness and share that information with our customers, demonstrating that we were maintaining our commitments. These steps laid the foundation for critical shifts in how we were approaching our work that remain in place today.

During this period, I learned how time-consuming effecting change can be. It was difficult to manage it and other aspects of my portfolio well, even with the help of my leadership team. I was pushed to recognize this fact by one of our outside consultants, who gently noted that it was not realistic for me to serve as a project lead. Recognizing these facts required a bit of letting go on my part, because I was excited about the model and wanted to play a very direct role in moving it forward. However, for the model to succeed, it needed dedicated leadership, which we transferred to one of my special assistants. We also created a separate, smaller "design team" made up of select leaders, my special assistant, staff, and our outside consultant. This group's purpose was to advise the leadership team on the project, oversee coordination of the online tool, create a project map to help track implementation, and develop metrics for evaluating the project's effectiveness.

NAVIGATING TRANSITION

Just as we were getting ready to launch the new protocol, a new agency head was appointed. Given the amount of resources directed toward this initiative, it was important that our new leader agreed that it made sense to move forward. Coincident with the change in leadership, I also saw an opportunity to leverage the effort by adding staff to each team from two other divisions that supported K–12 work.

The new superintendent enthusiastically supported the model and also liked the idea of including other divisions in the effort. He felt that the model could significantly improve the agency's performance and asked that we present our plan to the Mayor. My colleagues in the other divisions also expressed interest in learning about the effort and how it could support their work.

We created a cross-divisional training session opened by the superintendent, who shared the transformational impact he believed the work could have.

Facilitators led the teams through several activities designed to help them learn more about the model and the functions of the three divisions. Team members reviewed data, learned about problem-solving processes, and conducted an in-depth analysis of one of their assigned LEAs.

Fullan (2002) notes that "coherence is an essential component of complexity and yet it can never be completely achieved" (p. 18). As the training unfolded, it became clear that we had been overly ambitious in our agenda—there was too much content and not enough time for discourse. Some activities felt disconnected from others, and participants who had less foundational knowledge may have struggled to find a connection to their work.

Evaluations from the event were revealing. While many felt overwhelmed by the concepts and activities in which they engaged, the majority spoke positively about the experience. Several participants noted that it was the first time they spoke directly with their peers about their work—a sobering thought. Others felt uncertain about what we were doing and asked for more clarity. Yet fewer participants than expected raised concerns about time constraints and work assignments. It seemed that we had lit a spark.

In the months that followed, the cross-division teams met monthly to learn more about the details of their work and their assigned LEAs. Challenges with maintaining momentum grew over time, however, as the demands of people's day-to-day obligations caused conflicts with scheduling. We wrestled with meeting attendance within our own team and had even more difficulty engaging staff from other divisions. Complicating matters further, the leader of one of the divisions departed during this time, and the leader of another felt it necessary to focus on reactive problem solving rather than proactive planning, which to him felt like an unaffordable luxury. I continued to make a case for the importance of the model to the superintendent and my colleagues, but we were starting to lose traction. Around this time, one of my directors expressed the need to change course and return our focus to special education. She indicated that she and some of her colleagues were frustrated by inconsistent attendance from other divisions, which she felt was undermining the model's effectiveness. By including other divisions, we had diluted focus without benefit.

Once again, I was faced with an unpleasant reality. My efforts to persuade my immediate colleagues of the power of the model had worked in the abstract, but I felt as if I were fighting against a somewhat chaotic and reactive culture within the agency. After deliberation, I realized that refocusing the effort on what I could control (i.e., my division) made the most sense. Fortunately, around this same time, the superintendent initiated agency-wide strategic planning. I put forth an argument for combining the existing elementary and secondary education division, whose leader had recently departed, with the division of special education, and he agreed to combine these functions in a single division. In addition to the many benefits of combining resources in this manner, I saw an opportunity to get the model's expanded scope back on a more definitive track.

Before the second year started, we needed to speak with representatives from LEAs to make sure that what we were planning would be helpful and effective. In our meetings, we heard brutal facts (Collins, 2001) about how the agency was viewed and what LEAs thought we needed to address most urgently. Some representatives felt that the agency and its responses to inquiries were not always helpful; they expressed confidence in just a handful of individuals whose names were circulated among the school community. Perhaps for these reasons, we heard skepticism about whether the proposed consultation model would effectively serve LEAs. Representatives were most concerned with the agency getting its core work right. LEAs also shared their appreciation that we were being thoughtful about our role and asking for input.

The challenges of creating a single K–12 division and the feedback we received from LEA leaders contributed to determining that we were not ready to launch the consultation model in year 2. Instead, we continued to work on building staff knowledge and supporting the use of the expanded online tool. That same year, the relatively new superintendent announced his imminent departure, and the agency underwent yet another transition.

When the new superintendent arrived, I shared information about the model's progress and the powerful role I felt it could play within the agency. The new superintendent appreciated the intent of the model but felt that it would make most sense to narrow the scope of the consultative component toward supporting new charter LEAs. We adjusted the scope of the model accordingly, focusing on one cross-agency team supporting new charter schools in their planning year and in their first year of operation.

CONCLUSION

As leaders, we are expected to solve problems—to know answers when others don't. I knew that our agency and division needed to be more effective in helping LEAs. This effort highlights the tension between having a clear view of a model in the abstract and facing real challenges in its implementation.

I learned some valuable lessons from this effort. The agency had a history of high turnover at the top (eight superintendents in 9 years), and several assistant superintendents left during this period. Changes in leadership often required renegotiation of the project, causing significant losses in momentum. Upon reflection, I could have taken more care with new colleagues and agency leadership to nurture a shared understanding and cultivate buy-in. Additionally, the investment of time and effort to effect this change was larger than I had foreseen. I learned that it is important to plan for some unforeseen circumstances and include a reasonable buffer of time and resources based upon the nature of the project. Lastly, I would have solicited input from LEAs much sooner. More generally, project planners should engage any key participants early in the process.

Many might question whether this project was entirely successful. True, it was not implemented as first envisioned. At the same time, the changes were the result of asking questions and listening to other perspectives: This is the essence of leadership through inquiry.

Further, the effort did result in some exciting successes in the agency. Two core components of the model have been sustained and refined since their inception. First, the online support tool we initiated for special education has been adopted agency-wide. Second, the second component of the model was launched with new charter LEAs, which now receive dedicated consultation and support from a cross-agency team during their first-year planning and their first year of operation.

This effort spearheaded a fundamental change in how we work as a team. We regularly question how we are doing our work and what we need to do differently. We consult with LEAs and other stakeholders up front on new initiatives to make sure that what we are doing makes sense. We see evidence that these shifts are paying dividends. For example, 2 years ago, we launched a new monitoring approach. We asked every LEA who participated in our pilot year to respond to a survey about our effectiveness, and how the new model compared to prior experiences. We received significant positive feedback, but we also heard that we needed to improve how we organized the work and communicated about steps in the process. As a result, we met monthly to develop clearer procedures, strengthen our written communications, and ensure role clarity across the teams. This past year, we were pleased to see that LEAs felt we had markedly improved.

This work also enhanced the appreciation that leaders had of the capabilities and commitment of their staff. The expectation is that we all work to actively deepen our knowledge, share it with others, and learn from others.

Through this effort, I became more comfortable with uncertainty, a necessary attribute for managing significant change. I also learned that I needed to make myself vulnerable in order to lead well. Successful change is more likely to occur in an environment characterized by high levels of trust, one in which all can ask questions, challenge assumptions, and make and repair mistakes.

Leading from within a bureaucratic organization is inherently complicated. In this circumstance, I was a leader but also a middle manager within an agency in constant flux. How does one have a meaningful impact when situated in a complex, hierarchical landscape? It is certainly important to understand the needs of those we serve in order to effectively support and deliver services to them. But to be effective at changing how services are delivered, knowing customer needs is not enough. Leaders must also be adept at making a clear case for change, with superiors, colleagues, and direct reports. This requires understanding each group's unique relationship to the work, creating a "compelling vision" (Collins, 2001) for what needs to be changed, and intentionally carving out time for conversations that allow for reflection on practice and the creation of a collective willingness to try something different.

The pace of work in most education organizations is dizzying, but how do we know we are doing the right work? While there are many bright spots, successes are still far too limited after years of reform across the country, and great inequities linked to race, socioeconomic status, and other demographic characteristics persist. In fact, our data from this inquiry approach makes a strong case that we need to try something different. Perhaps if we spend more time in critical dialogue and "problem-posing" (Cochran-Smith & Lytle, 2009), we will get closer to our goal of ensuring that all children receive what they need to be successful in life. This is the untapped potential of inquiry-based leadership.

REFERENCES

Blythe, T., Allen, D., & Powell, B. (1999). *Looking together at student work.* New York, NY: Teachers College Press.

Cochran-Smith, M., & Lytle, S. L. (2009). *Inquiry as stance: Practitioner research for the next generation.* New York, NY: Teachers College Press.

Collins, J. (2001). *Good to great: Why some companies make the leap and others don't.* New York, NY: HarperCollins.

Fullan, M. (2002). The change leader. *Educational Leadership, 59*(8), 16–20.

Heifetz, R., Grashow, A., & Linsky, M. (2009). *The practice of adaptive leadership: Tools and tactics for changing your organization and the world.* Cambridge, MA: Harvard Business Press.

Spillane, J., Halverson, R., & Diamond, J. B. (2004). Towards a theory of leadership practice: A distributed perspective. *Journal of Curriculum Studies, 36*(1), 3–34.

CHAPTER 10

Life After the Zone

Marquitta T. Speller

Marquitta T. Speller is currently the executive director for secondary and collegiate programs at the Harlem Children's Zone (HCZ). Beginning in 2009, she served as the Director of Curriculum and Instruction and, shortly after, became the principal of HCZ's Promise Academy High School. In her current position, she oversees the Promise Academy High Schools, HCZ's College Success Office, and Career Services Team. Speller is also an adjunct professor at the College of Staten Island, and she teaches in the Penn Literacy Network. She received her doctorate in educational leadership from the University of Pennsylvania as well as a master's degree and her bachelor's degree from the University of Rochester.

In June of 2012, I applauded as all of my Promise Academy High School students graduated on time.* I stood on the stage and looked out at the crowd; I was satisfied. Happy, even. Each graduate had received multiple acceptance letters to colleges and universities throughout the country. Our first graduating class had fulfilled our mission's "promise." As the principal of the first Promise Academy High School, I was proud of what my team had accomplished. It is not too often that a school with our demographic accomplishes this goal. I felt that my job was done. Then, Thanksgiving came.

One of the top-performing students from the previous year's graduating class started showing signs of distress at college. First, it was trouble in a calculus class, even though she earned a top score on the advanced placement calculus exam she took in high school. Then she needed an extension for the paper that was due for her freshman writing class. This student never struggled with writing—this I knew for a fact. Prior to becoming the principal of the high school, I had been the assistant principal for the humanities department, and this young woman was in the advanced English class that I taught. Her state exam score for ELA was 98%. Yet writing a 10-page paper was new to her, and she just did not know what to say. "I mean, so they want me to say the same thing over and over again? I already made my point on the third page! What else am I supposed to say?" she confided.

*Please note that this does not include one student who entered our high school a full year behind in credits accumulated.

In fact, as students came back to visit during their breaks, I heard more comments of this nature. I started to learn more about the experiences that my students were having while in college, and that feeling of pride that I had in June was quickly evaporating. By December of that year, I started to wonder what had gone so wrong. Where had I failed as a leader? As more students shared similar stories about their college journey, I became obsessed with understanding the disconnect between high school and college. This was new territory for me. I never struggled in school, and college was no exception. I had assumed that since my students were able to graduate from high school on time, and get into college, they would be fine.

Promise Academy encapsulates the hopes and aspiration of Harlem Children's Zone (HCZ) and serves as a national exemplar for what low-income, minority students can accomplish when provided the range of resources available to more-privileged children. So, the difficulties some of our graduates were having as they transitioned to college challenged my belief that we had designed a program that would ensure the continuing success of all of our graduates.

I have worked at Harlem Children's Zone since 2009. I believe in its mission, and I work to ensure that the organization's vision comes to fruition. More importantly, I was born in Harlem and have deep roots in the community. I served as the principal for the students who graduated in 2012 and 2013. I know the students who tell their stories in this chapter well, having taught, mentored, reprimanded, consoled, and counseled all of them at some point. Beyond that, I have an insatiable appetite to get things right for every student, every time, no matter what. Teaching, for me, is a political act. It is my way of disrupting the status quo by providing the best experience possible for the young people with whom I work. I believe that every student should have access to a high-quality education that is rich with experiences and exposures that prepare them for life.

THE SETTING

I started my career as a teacher in a traditional New York City public high school and had great experiences in the different traditional public schools in which I worked, but I wanted to work in an environment that connected to the different needs of its community. When I was offered a position as assistant principal at Promise Academy, I thought it would be an ideal opportunity.

My school is like most charter schools in New York City, but the organization I work for is unique in its mission. Though the school shares some commonalities with other high-performing charter schools in the city, my school differs from them because of its partnership with the Harlem Children's Zone, a not-for-profit, multiservice organization that offers a variety of services to the Harlem community. HCZ's history revolves around a long-term goal to eradicate poverty in an area that is known nationally as the Black Mecca. The streets of Harlem have historically been used as a podium for influential leaders in the Black community, including Malcolm X, Adam Clayton Powell Jr., and members of the Black Panther Party. However, the spread of drugs into Harlem, specifically crack cocaine in the 1980s, resulted in significant deterioration in an already struggling community.

Statistics from the most recent state exams for grades 3–8 show that students in Harlem's Community School District 5 yield results that are significantly lower than the citywide average (schools.nyc.gov/Accountability/data/TestResults/ELAandMathTestResults). HCZ works to reroute students' academic trajectory from one of academic failure to one of academic engagement and success. After-school and community programs place strong emphasis on college and career readiness. All the students who attend the HCZ Promise Academy charter school in the heart of Central Harlem benefit from this focus.

The Harlem Children's Zone is in a unique situation because it works with youth from birth through college. Most students who enter Promise Academy for high school will have been with the organization since kindergarten or earlier. This gives HCZ an opportunity to create a K–12 experience for students who attend the charter school that is truly aligned with college enrollment and completion requirements, extending beyond what state requirements provide.

Embedded in the HCZ mission is the belief that a college degree is mandatory for economic prosperity. To fulfill this part of its mission, HCZ has adopted a "whatever it takes" attitude that functions as a mantra for employees of the organization. Our promise to parents—one I take seriously—is that their children will be admitted to and succeed in college. The goal of the organization is to create a "tipping point" in the neighborhood by surrounding children in an environment of caring, college-oriented people (Dobbie & Fryer, 2013). Staff members work assiduously to create a college-going culture in academic programs and in the Harlem community. Their commitment stems from the belief that communities and schools must be improved simultaneously in order to positively affect student achievement (Dobbie & Fryer, 2013). Because most of the students who participate in HCZ and Promise Academy programs are first-generation college-goers, supports have been put in place to help them navigate college life.

The inaugural cohort of students who graduated from the first Promise Academy in 2012 had attended the school since 6th grade. I was their principal. Our goal at the time was straightforward: 80% of students were expected to graduate from high school on time and immediately enroll in college. We were thrilled that students from the class of 2012 and beyond surpassed that goal with a 100% graduation rate and a 98% college acceptance rate.**

**College Success evaluation results for Harlem Children's Zone (HCZ) are tracked internally by the organization for the HCZ graduating classes of 2012 through 2016. More than 75% of those attending 4-year schools are on track to graduate within 6 years, far exceeding the national average for all students. The retention rates for HCZ graduates attending 2-year schools is three times that of Black students nationally, and 50% higher than White students.

Taking an Inquiry Stance—Listening to Graduates

For the past few years, I have created a space for students, staff, and the community to provide feedback on our current practices as a school. This started with my doctoral work that looked specifically at the transition our students made from high school to college (see Speller, 2015). I talked to former students and asked them to be forthcoming about where we fell short as a school community. I transcribed their responses and looked for cross-cutting themes; the results suggested a number of student challenges.

To get a more complete understanding of these themes I also surveyed 100 college students who had participated in HCZ's college outreach counseling program (for students attending other high schools in NYC). Their responses reiterated several of the themes that emerged from the interviews: difficulty with managing independent time and understanding differences in academic expectations; financial struggles; issues with family; and cultural shock from being in a new and completely different environment. My former students told mixed stories of excitement and dismay as they talked about the ways that they were attempting to navigate college life.

As I heard more and more of their stories, I became increasingly curious about the ways in which these graduates experienced the transition from high school to college. Many students face academic hurdles when they transition from high school to college. But students who are first-generation college-goers seem to face even greater obstacles. My students came from supportive environments, but they were all the first in their families to attend college immediately after graduating from high school. They had experienced varying degrees of success while in high school, but they told similar stories about the nature of their transition to college. The stories shared recurrent themes regardless of what college they attended and revealed aspects of each student's struggle to survive in a different world. In the pages that follow, I try to capture the voices of the graduates as they elaborate on these and other issues, make sense of and provide context for their messages, and consider what these issues may mean for Promise Academy.

Academic Expectations

All of the participants performed well in high school, but they experienced a new set of academic challenges when they entered college. The most apparent theme was how different the standards and expectations were for academic performance. One graduate, Sasha,[†] shared:

> The first semester, my GPA was bad. I cried when I got it back. I was so disappointed in myself. But I like didn't know what to do. I was like, "I don't know what to do." And I never failed a class in my life. And that's what made my GPA so low.

[†]Pseudonyms used to protect confidentiality of former students.

The expectations for the students attending more competitive schools were even higher. These students were accustomed to doing well in school and to being at the top of their class; however, they quickly learned that everyone else there was a star student in high school too. While learning how to deal with the academic and social pressures, they also had to come to terms with the reality that academic rigor increased significantly at these types of schools.

Managing Time; Learning to Study

Many of my students reported having poor study habits when they entered college. Another recent graduate, Lateema, explained:

> It was a big transition. Going to college I didn't know how to study. A lot of students don't. I didn't feel bad, but I realized I had to find a formula in order for me to obtain the information. I'm not happy about the amount of time I spend on studying.

Appropriate and productive use of independent time was a skill that many of the young people realized they did not possess. As I thought about it, I realized that during their time in high school, there had been few opportunities for students to study independently. Each minute of the day was carefully planned, with little to no room for creative use of independent time. Students had a study hall hour where they were expected to work independently on homework assignments or study for exams, but even that time was structured and teacher-supervised. Students were given 45 minutes each day for lunch, but mandatory tutoring for many high school students interrupted even that time. The high school staff spent quality time ensuring that they were ready to take and do well on state exams, but that required an incredible amount of guided support. They were not given opportunities to exercise organizational skills in ways that would prepare them to succeed on their own. There was no time that was not managed by an adult at Promise Academy. So, on reflection, it was no surprise that our graduates expressed an inability to manage their independent time effectively.

Adjusting to College

Promise Academy students had to adjust to life academically, socially, and emotionally, all of which were equally complicated. Looking back from college, the Promise graduates recognized that they were accustomed to being treated a certain way—one described it as "being babied." They were used to having extra time to complete assignments, receiving wake-up calls from staff, turning in work late with little consequence, and getting numerous opportunities to get something right. Life on a college campus was a major adjustment for them because things did not work like that anymore. Students shared stories about the ways in which this treatment paralyzed them when they entered college. Lateema explained:

> Honestly, I think when a student's grade is not where it should be you have to let them know. You have to be able to say, regardless of the kind of relationship you have with the student, "No makeup work." You can't give them the leeway not to produce something at a certain time. In college it's all about meeting deadlines. It's all about meeting the criteria. If you're not at college-level, you're going to fail.

My students were given plenty of opportunities to recover from mistakes when they were in high school. This was true for academic mistakes as well as disciplinary infractions. What this looked like at Promise Academy was that teachers were often encouraged to give students opportunities to make up assignments or do extra work to improve their grades.

This level of student support extended to other areas of the school experience as well. Students at Promise Academy were also provided with everything that they needed for school, including book bags, notebooks, pens, calculators, and school uniforms. One former student, Fatu, shared:

> Once I left HCZ, I was like, "Oh, we have to pay for things like books? Are you serious?" I was grateful but I didn't understand that we had to pay for things like books when we left. Promise has to stop making it easy for everything. Just prepare us for real life. No one gives you anything in the real world so don't give us everything here. I feel like going to college we weren't prepared for that. Just be real. I didn't like that.

The school's rationale was that providing the students with the tools that they needed would remove barriers and allow them to focus on learning. The staff at Promise Academy did not want students to experience failure or disappointment in ways that would damage their self-esteem, but we had not anticipated what this might mean for our students once such support ended.

The Knowledge Gap

Our students not only shared feelings of frustration about not being prepared for the adjustments they had to make while in college, they were equally frustrated by information that they were not exposed to while in high school but that other students seemed to know. They began to realize how circumscribed their experiences had been. Most of them had not spent much time outside of Harlem. Their knowledge of the world was limited to what they learned at home, on TV, on the streets, and in textbooks. For many of the participants, this was their first experience away from home and away from New York City.

Some of them were accustomed to doing well in high school and always knowing the right answers. They shared stories about the gaps in knowledge that they experienced when they entered college. I wondered whether so much time had been devoted to preparing students to do well on state exams that there had not been many opportunities for students to explore topics and ideas that did not fit into the structured curriculum culminating in the exams. Sasha confided:

> My knowledge gap was actually astonishing to me and I was like, "Wow, everyone is so far ahead of me." It's like starting a race on a 200 but they start at the 100-meter mark. And I was running the 800 right before that. That's how it felt. How were we supposed to know this stuff and these words on this list?. . . The professor was like, "Oh, well that's supposed to be prior knowledge. . . . I can't believe you don't know this." I'm like, "I can't believe it either."

Another student, LaToya, also noted:

> My first semester I took political science and a lot of it was basically information you should know. The professor kept saying, "You should know this already," and I was so embarrassed that I didn't know it. There was another girl in my class who came from like a small charter school in New York City, too. We were both confused. Of course, we're the only two Black people in the class.

What resonated in the stories that my students shared was their feeling that they could never catch up. Sasha's track and field analogy painted a vivid picture of a person trying to keep up with—not even win—a race after starting late. As she talked about her experience, it was evident that her feelings of embarrassment, coupled with the professor's disbelief that she did not know the information, made her feel more like an outsider on her campus. Similarly, as LaToya stated, she was embarrassed by what she did not know. Her professor's comments of "You should know," coupled with the fact that she and the other Black student were the only ones who did not know the information, had a negative impact on her confidence.

The Challenges of Promise Academy's Curriculum

The stories that the graduates shared and the themes that emerged from them called into question the ways in which their high school experience had prepared them for college. It gradually became clear to me that the K–12 curriculum at Promise was designed to get students through high school, but not necessarily through college. Students were required to earn a certain number of credits in specific subject areas, but there were not many opportunities for students to take elective courses, and there were very few Advanced Placement courses offered.

Sasha's experience in college caused her to question the level of preparation that she had in high school. The academic expectations at her college were high, and she expressed feeling unprepared for the challenge:

> I was in a crisis. This school did not prepare me for this kind of work. I feel like this school did the best they could do. Like, let's be honest. The majority of the school, well the kids that I graduated with, weren't going to a school like mine. Most of them were going to a CUNY or community college, and that's what I feel the school prepared us for. What else would I expect? The best you could have done was like split those people off. People who you knew were going to good [sic] schools. But even then, it still couldn't prepare us for college. It's almost impossible.

Sasha's observation raised several questions, most importantly how well Promise prepares its graduates for a range of college environments.

Race—Being Black

Issues of race also surfaced in the stories of all my students as they navigated campus life with their peers and their professors. The participants had teachers in high school who were from all different backgrounds, but to my knowledge they never expressed feeling as though a teacher had been racist toward them. Taylor talked about experiences that she had with a professor whom she deemed racist. This particular professor spoke to the Black students in ways that Taylor perceived as being much more critical than White students and which she found offensive:

> I felt like she was racist. And throughout the whole semester I struggled with her. She seemed to have issues with all of the Black kids. You know, because she was one of those strict professors, but only with the Black kids. I really struggled with her.

Taylor knew that there was something different and, in her opinion, wrong about the way that Black students were treated by this professor. Her story reinforced my sense that Promise students were rarely in situations where they had to confront issues associated with racism. As a result, they never developed the competencies necessary to deal with issues of this nature. Students were not aware of the inequalities that existed in their own city because they rarely ventured outside of their neighborhoods, and many never had to deal with an adult who was blatantly racist toward them. They lived their lives in Harlem and did not think about race issues on a broader scale.

When it came to dealing with race issues, there was a general feeling of "not belonging" or "not feeling welcomed" in college that the recent graduates shared. For Curtis, that feeling manifested in the form of intimidation:

> There were a lot of students and I guess I kind of got frightened a little. I feel like when you're Black and you're in a college like that, you are already

> different. I guess I didn't want to be that one kid that stands out even more. I didn't feel like being the stereotypical Black student. I didn't want to be that kid.

The isolation presented a dauntingly new context:

> During orientation weekend, you meet a lot of Black students. When you get to class, it's a totally different story. Sometimes it'll be like six Black kids in a class of 300. So, I just didn't want to be that one kid. I don't know, I guess I was just scared that first year.

By his account, Curtis did not want to fall victim to what has been called "stereotype threat." Cohen and Garcia (2005) discussed the concept of a "collective threat," meaning that the actions of an individual will reinforce the negative stereotypes that exist about that particular group. Curtis was concerned with standing out as the "Black kid." I asked him to explain what impact being the only Black student in a room would have on him. He talked about not wanting to be judged or criticized. His fear was that people would view him as a person who did not really belong.

What stood out most from my inquiries with former students was that during our interviews, Promise graduates all appreciated the support that they received from their HCZ's College Success Office counselors, college personnel, family, and friends. Despite the obstacles they faced in life, or during the transition to college, each participant was clear about the need and desire to persevere. Though many Promise graduates have encountered challenges while in college, the overwhelming majority have persisted.

STRUGGLING TO RETHINK OUR ASSUMPTIONS

My decision to work in a community with Black and Brown people who are living in less than ideal conditions came out of a sense of purpose. Getting it right is important to me. The children believe us when we say that we will help them have a better life. While other factors may be beyond my control, I have to make sure that the things that are within my control are done well. There are plenty of things that we did and do very well as a school. But I know that we can do better.

That was apparent from the stories our former students told—stories of excitement and dismay as they attempted to navigate college life. Their stories raised questions for me about whether and how our current practices prepare, mentor, and support students, as well as mitigate the personal and familial demands that challenge their ability to have a positive experience. Were our efforts sufficient? As I considered what I had heard and learned, I recognized that my leadership challenge was to synthesize the "data" into student-generated recommendations that would facilitate our program development. I concluded that their recommendations to us were clear and direct, and could be expressed in manageable terms:

- Push Us; Expose Us
- Let Us Fail
- Support Us
- Let Us Grow

The students' direction was clear; moving forward would require revisiting some of the assumptions our leadership team had made.

"No nonsense" schools like KIPP, Success, and Promise Academy tend to encourage an environment where faculty and staff do "whatever it takes" in the hopes of ensuring that their students are prepared to meet the challenges of college life. Students have access to unlimited support and services that they do not have to seek out on their own. Teachers and administrators believe that students from struggling communities can succeed, a belief that manifests in many ways. The dilemma is that educators sometimes have a hard time balancing "doing whatever it takes" and doing too much. Not doing enough results in students receiving failing grades. Doing too much results in students' inability to develop coping mechanisms that are the cornerstone for success. Even with all the systems in place, the adults who are directly responsible for the success of the students have to determine what is needed, including the right dose of support, for the students to thrive. Our graduates' feedback provided guidance for us (and potentially for other educators) regarding what could be done to serve them better.

Push Us; Expose Us

The graduates talked about the need for a more rigorous high school experience. Those students who had an opportunity to participate in pre-college courses and exposures reported feeling better prepared for the transition than those who did not have that opportunity. They made it clear that they were not challenged enough in high school. They never had to study for long periods of time, they barely took notes that were not already prepared for them and placed on the board, and they were not given many opportunities to take elective courses that pushed their thinking. They were in the habit of taking exams that required them to memorize facts, but not think critically or analytically. Recognizing these shortcomings, the graduates were adamant that they should have had more opportunities to take Advanced Placement courses, for example, and when necessary, the support needed to succeed in them. They wanted to have been challenged more, to have been pushed to take greater academic risks. This was a hard lesson for us to receive as educators.

Let Us Fail

The price of failure for students from communities like Harlem can be significant; there is not the space and time for recovery that exists for students with more means. However, from our students' point of view, not providing space and opportunities for failure results in their inability to develop strategies for navigating future obstacles. Additionally, and as a result, some said that they also needed more socio-emotional supports.

Support Us

The wellness issues that some of these graduates had were barriers to their persistence and suggested the need for helping them learn how to access mental health and wellness services at college. In addition, as students dealt with issues of acceptance and rejection from family, friends back home, and people from college, they found themselves negotiating uncomfortable terrain. It was not always clear to them where they could turn for help, or that seeking help was an acceptable thing to do.

Let Us Grow

A common theme was the graduates' perception that they were coddled too much while in high school. The graduates made it clear that what we did in the Promise Academy K–12 setting did not encourage independence. The former students stated that they would have benefited both from opportunities to fail and from opportunities for exploration—to go where they had not been before, to learn how to navigate on their own.

ACKNOWLEDGING THE IMPORTANCE OF LEADING FROM AN INQUIRY STANCE

Adopting an inquiry stance in my interactions with our graduates, asking questions, not being defensive, both allowed and required me to listen carefully to and make sense of the stories I was being told, and to figure out how to share those stories in our community in ways that made their messages the impetus for accomplishing our mission. As I revisited their stories, looking for unifying themes, I developed the four recommendations from the graduates I've listed above—which then framed our planning, redesign, and implementation. As the leadership team moved forward, teachers, parents, and administrators were repeatedly asked whether our responses to the graduates' recommendations would push students and broaden their experience in ways related to the demands of college; teach them how to access both wellness and academic supports; allow them to experience failure without damaging their life chances; and provide opportunities for growth and independence?

Without going into a detailed description of the many changes we made, the most obvious and significant was allowing for more explicit collaboration between the two HCZ high schools, Promise I and Promise II, so that students have the opportunity to take a greater variety of courses after meeting certain criteria. One of the campuses now offers our advanced STEM curriculum, and the other, a few blocks away, offers the advanced humanities courses. As a result, students now walk back and forth between the two campuses, learning to manage unsupervised time as they will need to do in college. Another advantage is that by combining the two schools' core content curriculum departments, we can offer a greater range of courses in math, English, the sciences, and social studies, including many more AP courses. The outcome: Our current students have been extremely enthusiastic about the change, and report feeling more independent and more responsible. We are in the initial stages of this change, and we anticipate making additional modifications as time goes on.

And finally, as I watch our school evolve, I take satisfaction in knowing that our program changes have been driven by our deep concern for and commitment to our students, that they recognize this and continue to be candid in their feedback, and that we can in good conscience say that at Promise reform is student-driven, not dictated by policy.

REFERENCES

Cohen, G. L., & Garcia, J. (2005). "I am us": Negative stereotypes as collective threats. *Journal of Personality and Social Psychology*, 89(4), 566–582.

Dobbie, W., & Fryer, R. (2013). Getting beneath the veil of effective schools: Evidence from New York City. *American Economic Journal: Applied Economics*, 5(4), 28–60.

Speller, M. T. (2015). *Life after the Zone: A retrospective account of students from the Harlem Children's Zone* (Doctoral dissertation). Retrieved from ProQuest Dissertations & Theses Database. (Order No. 3746346).

CHAPTER 11

Our Community, Our Schools, and Our Money

Stephen Benson

Stephen Benson is an educational consultant who formerly served as an assistant superintendent in Western Pennsylvania and then was appointed superintendent of a rural central Pennsylvania district. He began his career as a jazz musician, became a high school music educator and then an ISO 9001 Quality Systems Certified Lead Auditor analyzing, auditing, and writing district policies, procedures, and practices. Collectively, these experiences had much to do with his approach to district leadership. Benson earned his doctorate in educational leadership from the University of Pennsylvania, his master's degree from the University of Miami, and a bachelor's degree from Berklee College of Music.

Halfway through the school year, the administration, board, and teachers of a historically fiscally-stable district realized they had a serious financial problem. The then board president, along with the business manager and superintendent, had spent the substantial cash reserves, which forced the district to borrow $1.5 million to continue paying the bills. By the end of summer, the superintendent, assistant superintendent, business manager, and more than 50 recently hired employees were gone, one school was closed, supply orders were cancelled, and property taxes were considerably increased.

Shortly after, with no community or district input, I was selected by a majority of the board members to lead the district. They told me my skill set, particularly my financial know-how, stood apart from the other applicants' and that they thought I could help stem the financial crisis. I quickly learned that the problems in the district were more than budgetary. The school closure caused by the budgetary turmoil had set the district reeling. Losing a K–6 building in this 222-square-mile rural district in central Pennsylvania extended travel time by up to an hour daily for hundreds of students, changed well-established routines, and displaced local civic activities. Angry citizens and parents came to lodge their complaints during every board meeting.

Traveling the 150 miles from where I lived with my wife and three sons to begin a new job in this community, several things were apparent to me immediately.

Being a White middle-class male seemed to make me a fit for this 97% White, mostly middle-class district led by an all-male administration. However, lifelong residents and newcomers alike told me not being born in the area meant I would never be accepted. Additionally, in their view, my having graduated from an Ivy League college meant that I could not be trusted. Even aside from my outsider status, the scandal in the school administration meant that distrust ran rampant throughout the district and community. As the fourth superintendent in 6 years, my resume became the document most frequently requested through the district's open records policy. Moreover, inspired by the mismanagement of the district, leaders of a recently created community group, apparently informed and prompted by several teachers, consistently expressed distrust of district leadership.

The district was below the fifth percentile statewide in family income and college graduation rates. While a number of people seemed unaware of the turmoil in the school district, some observed in silence, and many other people seemed unwilling to speak their minds for fear of what would be said about them. A few individuals came to dominate board meeting public discussion time. The vocal people dictated the discourse by continuously demanding that their concerns be addressed, whether they were about bus routes, personnel decisions, or building conditions.

I tried not to take the public complaints by angry citizens personally. I listened carefully to understand their positions because they felt wronged and I empathized with them. Lamentably, my quiet and inquiring approach frustrated them. They were angry and wanted to fight, not talk, about what the previous leadership did to their children, schools, and taxes. Privately, some people informed me that they appreciated my willingness to listen to their thoughts and include their insights in decisions; this produced many allies. However, not all were pleased with me continually asking questions that some said made them feel challenged or threatened, when all they wanted were answers. I explained that the district could provide more satisfying responses if we had a better understanding of what they were thinking, and the only way to find that out was by asking questions and listening carefully to their responses.

EARLY INQUIRIES

Before becoming superintendent, I had spent years as a jazz musician, knowing the tunes we were going to play, but deeply aware of the need to listen to my bandmates and build on their improvisations as we progressed through a song. As the new leader of an unfamiliar band, I drew on that experience. In my mind, taking an inquiry stance as superintendent was much like playing jazz—having a preliminary sense of where an inquiry might go, but aware of the tension between acting from my authority as the leader and positioning myself as the learner—not knowing where our inquiry would take us, but respecting and trusting the process.

My secretary was a major ally in our daily inquiries about what we were trying to accomplish and, more important, why. She scheduled my meetings with parents and community members. She also joined us to take notes, which we reviewed with our guests after each meeting to ensure accurate documentation. Some people expressed their feeling that my questions were "fancy talk," a trick to confuse or take advantage of people who just wanted straight answers. In response, I committed to taking time to explain the reasoning behind my questions.

During one meeting, an upset mother began crying, relieved that I supported her daughter's position regarding a conflict with a teacher. After the parent left, my secretary commented that people often came in furious and left feeling good; this was not something this community had experienced. We discussed whether this shift could be attributed to taking an inquiry approach: start with a question, listen carefully, seek clarification, stay open to possibilities without judging, and focus on creating mutually satisfying solutions.

Over time, as administrators and teachers began to experience positive outcomes with inquiry, they wanted to learn more; they invited me to meetings, particularly with students they found challenging. They witnessed how quickly these students would engage in productive dialogue when respectfully asked thoughtful questions. But the administrators and teachers also voiced two concerns. First, they asked, "Where do the questions come from?" They said that when they listened to me, the questions made sense, but it was only upon reflection that they could detect the logic leading to the resolution. They struggled to predict or form the questions on their own.

I suggested some ways to formulate inquiry-based questions: Try not to confuse facts with your personal beliefs and values; be willing to listen to and understand others before judging. Ask questions that you are genuinely interested in to help learn what the other person thinks. I explained that I had found these techniques helpful in forming a shared understanding of the situation. When you uncover others' value lenses, then you can plan a resolution respecting those values. As an example of one aspect of this approach, I told the following story: A student became violent when his teacher called him stupid. I asked him what he does outside of school, and he meticulously explained how pigs are born, raised, slaughtered, carved, and sold—all of which he did on his farm. I respected his competence and he responded in kind.

The second concern administrators and teachers shared focused on how people became anxious when being asked questions. I acknowledged that reaction and said that some people are comfortable with polite, surface-level conversation, but if you genuinely pursue a deeper understanding of what someone thinks, it can sometimes be perceived as rude, intrusive, or threatening. The only response I had was to tell them that it takes time, sincerity, and consistent caring action to build the necessary trust that would enable people to feel comfortable enough to function as equal partners in an inquiry. My follow-up questions with the above-mentioned student, for example, helped to show the young man my sincere interest in his competence and provided a model for his teacher in building respectful relationships with students.

Beyond those two issues, I explained to this group the idea of non-zero-sum thinking to move them from binary—win/lose; right/wrong; yes/no—managers to acting as authentic leaders. I encouraged them to expand their understanding of the person they are speaking with and the dynamics of the situation.

The interest of the administrators in inquiry grew as the district began to transform many of its practices. A seismic shift occurred when the board approved 2 hours of professional development (PD) every Wednesday afternoon for all instructional employees in the district. Following each PD session, administrators would meet beginning at 3:30 p.m. to discuss the progress of their inquiries. No one was required to stay, but nearly everyone did—every week. Seeing the level of engagement, I did not want to limit our time; however, out of respect I said that we would stop the meetings at 5:30. Meetings would often go on until people realized the time, often as late as 7:00 p.m. I encouraged administrators to miss a meeting if they needed to attend family events, but interest was strong, and most meetings had 100% attendance. The PD sessions continued for 3 years, and the administrator inquiry group continued until my departure several years later.

THE SITUATION AND ISSUES

State test results indicated that the district functioned well below average, with at least one school achieving below the fifteenth percentile. The district was recovering from the loss of one seventh of its workforce and all of its money, and two of its five schools were in desperate need of renovations.

Based on those conditions, I defined my job as focusing all of us in this fragmented community—students, parents, other residents—on an all-encompassing integrated vision of "high student achievement" and ensuring that we dedicated all resources toward this goal. I consistently reinforced the vision with three questions, in writing and in conversations, which I tried to raise at every meeting:

1. What do you want for the students in the district?
2. How do you plan to achieve what you want?
3. What role do you play in achieving what you want?

I pleaded with people to come together through the school board's leadership to create a shared vision for the future of the district. My mantra was, "Please discuss what you want and how you want to accomplish it." I encouraged them to start by listening to each other, finding points of agreement, adding to the solution, and continuing to improve.

The difficulty in progressing with this inquiry was evident during board meetings. I begged them privately and in public to discuss what they wanted for the students, but month after month, several members came to the meetings and complained about different things that were not being done to their satisfaction, without expressing what they wanted done in advance. Everything, it seemed, was a reaction to something a friend or neighbor told them. Frustrated, I asked them to say one thing they wanted me to work on tomorrow to improve our schools. After one member expressed her opinion, it became apparent to other board members that they did not share the same view and needed to participate in the inquiry, not leave it up to individual voices to speak for the group. That seemed to shift the discourse to begin building a common vocabulary and set of ideas that would enable us to have productive dialogues at board meetings. I engaged them in discussions about leadership concepts, approaches, and theories, and how they directly related to our situation. Aware of the varied strong feelings in the community and on the board, I would carefully frame the ideas around issues we were dealing with that month. Frequently, I would present specific district information or write short book summaries, then distribute them to anyone who expressed interested. I wrote many detailed emails to the board, teachers, the entire district, and the media, preparing them for, or further explaining, ideas that I presented. I received myriad responses to the emails from a wide range of readers. Many were messages of approval, but there were also complaints from some people saying they could not keep up with everything I was writing. During one period, six of the nine board members (four of whom were retired teachers) refused to use computers, including email, which greatly impeded my information-sharing efforts. Additionally, the public was not pleased when they learned that mailing the information along with the board agendas was costing over $100 per month and that board members were not opening the packets until they arrived at the public meeting. The problem for me was that I could not find another way to provide sufficient information to effectively engage in the monthly inquiries needed to improve decisions that were costing taxpayers millions of dollars.

RESEARCH

After hours of conversations with numerous constituents, I wrote and disseminated summaries of many books with content directly responding to their concerns. For instance, in *Hollowing Out the Middle* by Carr and Kefalas (2010), the authors identified four categories of young people in rural communities: Achievers, Stayers, Seekers, and Returners. The Achievers in the book (and in this district) were afforded positive attention and support from teachers, enabling them to leave the community through college, never to return. This book was relevant to my district since there had been a dramatic growth in Achievers through improved curricula. Many district parents had become anxious that their children would not stay in the community to take care of them as they and generations of their families had done before. This resulted in them construing their children's striving for better opportunities as a kind of betrayal.

Another challenge, demonstrated during several professional development sessions, was that many teachers had low expectations for the Stayers. To surface the point, I had teachers write the initials of five students on a piece of paper, then asked them to indicate what they saw each student doing when they were 25. The responses: on welfare, in prison, driving a truck, and working in fast food. There were a few professionals, such as teachers and nurses, and a few tradespeople. The teachers were not troubled by the similarity of their assumptions with teachers in the failed communities described in the book. They were convinced that their issues were unique, maintaining that others could not possibly comprehend the depth of the community's problems or provide any meaningful solutions.

What the community saw as my greatest weakness, a lack of history in the district, I perceived as my greatest strength. I had no issues with anyone in the community. From my "outsider"' perspective, the fragmented decisions being made based on feelings passed down through generations were related to the precipitous decline in student population and deterioration of the overall community.

Book summaries informed the board, district, and community that they were not alone; other communities faced similar challenges and, most importantly, some overcame their difficulties by studying the facts and taking action. Unraveling fact from fiction about the district's situation mattered, but deciding how to lead distrustful people from financial ruin and low academic achievement to success was an imperative. Determined and confident that following an inquiry approach would lead to success, I created multiple inquiry groups. For example, I met with all the K–6 math teachers by grade level for 3 hours each month to first improve, then completely redo, the math curriculum. I met with all grade 7–8 and 9–12 math teachers for a full day once a month and for more days during the summer. I set up comparable inquiry groups that worked for years on Language Arts, then groups for every other area: Special Education, School Counselor, Title I, custodian, and school cooks groups.

We were guided by the three overarching questions, asked follow-up questions pertinent to the settings, and initiated conversations about leadership approaches. I was part of every group, initially to model inquiry and later as a participant. What most superintendents do during the day, I did in the evening, enabling me to interact with students and employees all day.

DOING A SIMULATION WITH THE BOARD

During one public board meeting I brought eight paper lunch bags filled with various Tinkertoy pieces, and asked the board if they were willing to play a "Barbell Game." We put eight chairs in two groups of four back-to-back, asked board members and one administrator to take a seat, and handed each of them a bag of Tinkertoys. Before the meeting I showed two board members exactly how the barbells needed to be constructed and asked if they would each lead one of the two teams; they agreed. I explained to everyone that the point of the exercise was to make as many barbells as fast as you can. I asked if they knew what a barbell looked like, and they all said yes. The procedure was for the first person in each group to hand one Tinkertoy to the person to their right; that person could add or subtract one piece, then would hand it to the next person and so on until it was handed to the team leader who could only accept or reject it. If it was unacceptable, it was handed back to the first person to continue around the group again. I asked if there were any questions. There were none. The audience was to observe and document what was said and done by the participants. I put the timer on and told both teams to begin. At the end of round one, neither team had built a single barbell.

Before beginning round two, I stressed that during this round they needed to do whatever was necessary to build the barbells. Again, I asked, are there any questions for your team leader or me? In previous experiences (having done this activity before as a consultant), people usually asked the leader what a barbell was supposed to look like, an absolutely required piece of information. No one from these teams asked, and the leaders never offered. Other groups turned their chairs around facing each other, instead of back-to-back as I placed them, and dumped all the pieces on the floor between them and built the barbells; not these teams. Tensions began to rise, and not a single barbell was constructed during the second round either.

When the timer ended round two, I showed each team a barbell and suggested they turn around and work together. In less than one minute both teams accomplished what they could not do in the previous ten. We spent 20 minutes processing the experience and relating it to situations in our district. Some of the observations they made included:

1. Without having a clear understanding of the vision, a lot of time and energy was wasted becoming frustrated and angry. Their conclusion: There is value in creating a shared understanding of what we wanted to accomplish.
2. The lack of anyone asking questions was worrisome. They were discouraged by not knowing the goal, and reluctantly agreed that asking questions was probably a good strategy. They evidently feared this admission would appear to support the inquiry approach as practiced by the superintendent.
3. They were disappointed that they did not think to turn their chairs around and work together. When they did, they began to experience the value of collaboration in creating wholeness in a fragmented environment.

It was now time for all of us, including me, to apply what we were learning to the adaptive problems the district was facing. Every step taken to create wholeness required many synchronized inquiries into disparate elements of the district. The leadership team was beginning to assume some responsibility for the inquiries and was reminded to always begin with what is best for attaining high student achievement. We dialogued about every curricular area, teacher capacity to teach new or different curricula, teacher instructional practices, professional development opportunities and session content, special education service delivery, the role of cooks and custodians in building a learning organization, and—the issue that involved the entire community—the kind of facilities we needed to most effectively provide the education we wanted.

THE BUILDING INQUIRY

A facilities study completed prior to my arrival provided estimates for the renovation of two of our five schools, an option that in my opinion was not a wise choice given the outmoded designs of the buildings. I suspected that building a new modern facility would cost no more than renovating, but the public did not seem to trust that the district could construct a better building for the same dollar amount as renovating. Additionally, they felt one building had historical significance for the community, and they were still distressed by the closing of another school the previous year. This scenario presented the perfect opportunity for a community-wide inquiry.

Working collaboratively with varied employees, we convinced the board to create a committee to study all building and grade configurations. Using the phrase, "It's about our community, our schools, and our money," we advertised for people to sign up to be one of 23 members on a committee representing the board, administrators, teachers, parents, business owners, community activists, and community members with no affiliation with the schools. Once the committee members were elected from all the applicants, we held our first and most challenging meeting to develop dialogue skills. I continually pushed back to the first question of our inquiry, "What do we want for the students?" All committee members were accustomed to zero-sum leadership where people argued, and the strongest personality won, compelling the others to conspire against them. Each member came with an agenda and wanted to win; several agendas were diametrically opposed. For example, one community activist did whatever she could to keep the junior high building open in the downtown area, including sabotaging the group and personally attacking individuals in multiple media forums.

Committee members kept trying to change the question, saying "It does not matter what we want for students if we cannot pay for it. Therefore, the topic must be money." I was unbending, firm, that in my role as facilitator, I sometimes had to exercise authority to create the conditions for inquiry. "We will not talk about money until we talk about what is best for students," I often stated. I appreciated that most of the people assumed I would spend liberally, as did previous administrations. However, the truth was—and it took several years for everyone to learn—that I was the most fiscally conservative person on the committee. I was committed to not raising taxes while building a new school, and I knew it was realistic because I saw how much money was wasted throughout the district.

We held more meetings in each of the schools, including guided tours. No one could ignore the buckets scattered around the junior high school collecting dripping water from innumerable roof leaks. The public's accusation was that the building was not properly maintained, but the fact was that the district went many years past the life expectancy without replacing the roof. Repairs were made repeatedly at great cost with unsatisfying results. The electrical and heating systems, windows, floors, ceilings, auditorium, gymnasium, cafeteria, offices, and classrooms should have been upgraded years ago. The issue was long-term, capital budget planning, not maintenance.

The meetings included presentations of student enrollment projections and history, building capacities and grade configurations, the heights and location of bathroom and cafeteria facilities for 5-year-olds, green areas around schools, play areas, parent and bus access areas, and specific classroom facilities, such as sinks, lockers, or storage areas. This information focused the conversations about what we wanted for students. Should elementary students have access to a science laboratory? Should we keep the "cafegymatorium" and limit student access to a gymnasium to a few hours daily when the space was not being used as a cafeteria? What kind of music and art education do you want for all students? Do you want a library in each school? What purpose will it serve? What grade levels should be in each building? We had hundreds of questions we needed to consider thoughtfully. Changing lifelong beliefs about what schools were, and what they could be, challenged many minds and had huge dollar implications.

During our second meeting, we agreed to split the committee into three subgroups balanced in terms of roles and personal views; each group would study different building and grade configurations. The district had six schools; five were occupied at that time. One group looked at possibilities if we kept five buildings, another group looked at consolidating into four buildings, and the third group considered three buildings. We set the parameters for the presentations that would take place at a public meeting. Each group needed to at least address the options provided in the professionally prepared feasibility study, create a pros and cons chart for each option, and then make a recommendation as to which configuration they thought would best serve the students, without allowing finances to influence their decision. The subgroups met on their own time to prepare their final presentations.

Throughout the extensive process we put stories in the media and dedicated pages on the district website to the materials, the feasibility study, meeting notes and dates, PowerPoint slides, survey results, and all related documents. We advertised and held well-attended open public meetings at the junior high school to listen to citizen concerns and to answer all their questions. A survey was mailed to every home in the district, from which we received a 33% return. Finally, the public was invited to an open forum where the subgroups presented their recommendations, and after listening to the public input, the board reached an agreement; we would pursue a four-building plan. From there we had many more meetings, continuing to involve all the constituent groups with the development of the education specifications and building designs. Beyond the public meetings, teachers in grades 5 through 8 (the grades affected by the building consolidation) were personally interviewed and asked to complete an in-depth survey, and attended meetings by department and then grade level. Cooks and custodians were interviewed, as were all others that we thought might have an idea.

Concurrent with the building meetings, I was leading inquiries into many other aspects of the district, engaging as many people as possible. The following investigations are included because the total financial savings realized by their outcomes completely offset all costs for building the new school.

1. *Can or should our cafeterias be self-sufficient?* When I arrived, the cafeterias cost the district a quarter of a million dollars yearly, and four of the five ran significant deficits. Meeting with the director of food services, the head cooks, and the custodians for hours each month led to proposals that improved efficiencies and greatly increased sales, particularly by serving breakfast in several locations in each building. The district expenditure was completely eliminated. Cooks took the lead role in helping us reach the goal by convincing students that a healthy breakfast could improve their day. Engaging the cooks was a tremendous benefit for our finances, but more importantly to the school environments. Cooks began greeting students every morning, offering encouragement, support, and a variety of food choices. Many students commented on how much they enjoyed being welcomed by the cooks in the morning.
2. *Should the district pay double insurance for couples because the employees were entitled to it?* Family health insurance cost the district more than 18,000 dollars per plan per year, and most married couples were doubly insured. That meant the district paid 36,000 dollars to cover the many married couples without adding any benefit to the employee. I met with administrators, board members, and union representatives for several hours on more than a dozen occasions to discuss the issue. Some district leaders and employees saw this as a moral issue, because every employee was entitled to insurance; others felt one spouse should willingly surrender coverage. I suggested paying one of the married employees 5,000 dollars in cash to forgo the idea of having double coverage, without diminishing the actual health benefits available to them. The non-zero-sum resolution came by shifting the issue from the moral realm into the business sphere where paying to buy out one spouse made the employee very happy and saved the district more than 650,000 dollars per year, which made the board and administrators very happy.
3. *Do independent special needs students benefit from having a Personal Care Assistant (PCA)?* Since special education teachers wanted help they would require a PCA when writing the Individual Education Plan (IEP), even for independent students. The high school graduates hired as PCAs were told to bring reading material because the job was mostly sitting and waiting to fulfill teacher requests. Showing teachers and parents that student growth

increased with independence, we eliminated a significant number of PCAs through attrition, only allowing them for students with a demonstrated need.

4. *What is the role and goal of special education?* I met with every special education teacher, all fulltime assistants, the Director of Student Services, and the Director of Human Resources for 2 hours every Wednesday afternoon over 4 months to rethink special education as providing necessary and appropriate services rather than as a separate program. Additionally, we maximized ACCESS fund by creating an arrangement where the district is reimbursed for medical services provided to qualified students, which realized a saving of over 300,000 dollars per year.

When the monies saved in the four items above were combined with the savings from closing one of the five schools (we would need fewer staff overall) and the expected reimbursement from the state on a new building project, we easily found the funds to construct a new state-of-the-art facility.

LESSONS LEARNED

As I reflect on this experience, I realize that in addition to everything previously discussed, over the tenure of my superintendency, leading from an inquiry stance was my core strategy for restructuring the district grade levels and schedules; returning the district to fiscal stability with the healthiest reserve in its history; purchasing and implementing new, totally aligned K–12 curricula; transforming instruction, thereby increasing student achievement scores on the state assessment; implementing an entirely new arts program providing music, visual arts, and poetry to elementary children daily; and providing 3 years of weekly professional development for staff—all without raising taxes. In 2015, *U.S. News & World Report* named the high school a Silver Medal School, after years of persistently low achievement.

If I were to take on another superintendency, I would continue to use an inquiry approach to leadership because it engages people in a thoughtful, constructive, democratic process, leading to well-considered decisions, and it can produce coherence, wholeness, and non-zero-sum results when implemented effectively. For me, implementing an inquiry approach to leadership was a professionally and personally inspiring experience.

REFERENCE

Carr, P. J., & Kefalas, M. J. (2010). *Hollowing out the middle: The rural brain drain and what it means for America.* Boston, MA: Beacon Press.

Conclusion

Leading with Eyes Wide Open

As we hope we conveyed in the introduction to this book, we are not suggesting that leading from an inquiry stance is the only way to understand problems in the world of leadership and practice. But we are also not implying that taking an inquiry stance on leadership is merely some kind of add-on or extension to what leaders do in the everyday act of leading. What seems most important is that the chapter authors' inquiries are integral to and integrated with their practices as leaders. We believe repositioning leadership in this way may open a new path, with the potential to suggest new foci for "leaderly" inquiry, to inspire new writers, and to encourage practicing leaders to write in response to the work of their local or distal colleagues. They may, in this manner, nurture a new, expanded discourse, generated by leaders themselves, about some of the most vexing and often invisible aspects of their important work.

REVISITING THE FRAMEWORK OF LEADING FROM AN INQUIRY STANCE

Across the chapters in this book, variously defined communities of inquiry within schools and systems function to uncover, articulate, and question assumptions about aspects of teaching, learning, schooling, and leadership itself. Leaders play key roles in imagining, supporting, and participating in these collaborative efforts to gather and analyze information that can assist in thinking differently about critical issues in practice, which in turn can lead to meaningful change. To foster equity requires a posture and a willingness to work both within and against the system, and can be understood as an ongoing process of questioning assumptions about the purposes of the existing system and raising difficult questions about educational resources, processes, and outcomes. The fundamental intent of leading from an inquiry stance is the desire to enhance the learning and life chances of students and the likelihood of their active participation in a diverse society.

Leadership in this sense builds on the notion of *inquiry as stance* (Cochran-Smith & Lytle, 1999, 2009), which foregrounds the role that practitioners can play, both individually and collectively, in generating local knowledge, re-envisioning and theorizing practice, forming and reforming communities of inquiry, as well as interpreting and interrogating the theory and research of others.

Perhaps most distinctive about this stance for leaders is the disposition to treat one's own practice as a site for intentional investigation and knowledge construction, so that knowledge-making as a leader is a pedagogic act emanating from a context of use, and, while local, can be connected to wider contexts. *Leading* from an inquiry stance thus reflects an expanded and, we argue, transformative view of leadership practice, encompassing students', teachers', co-workers', and leaders' ongoing investigations into the social, cultural, intellectual, relational, and political aspects of knowledge construction. This "expanded view of practice" supports leaders' efforts to generate new knowledge from the practice of leading itself, and thus has intrinsic interest and value for other school and system leaders, as well as for those who provide professional development and further education in leadership.

POTENTIAL IMPLICATIONS FOR THE FIELD

If we imagine more leaders embracing a leadership practice that shifts toward an inquiry stance, what implications might this have for the study and practice of educational leadership? Our answer as a field will only emerge as our collective inquiry grows. Even so, this could represent potential changes in dominant leadership practices—both locally and, ultimately, collectively—bringing with it four important and logically-related implications.

In brief, an inquiry stance embodies and supports a broad vision of educational leadership, one which may, in turn, require shifts in recruitment, preparation, and support, including a diversification of the disciplinary lenses incorporated in leaders' preparation. This, in turn, may imply significant changes in the institutional, political, and relational infrastructures of education and schooling. A more widespread adoption of leadership from an inquiry stance thus carries the potential to transform professional norms, particularly in regard to voice, collegial relationships, and perceived standing of educational leaders in community and public discourse.

Toward Repositioning Educational Leadership

As we see in the chapters of this volume, leading from an inquiry stance offers an alternative conception of educational leadership as a profession. In leading with eyes wide open to the complexity of local context, inquiry-based leadership broadens and deepens the leader's role, often shifting the balance between instrumental and adaptive foci. As shared by one of our contributing authors:

> As leaders, we are expected to solve problems—to know answers that others don't or to create them when others won't. In some ways the most courageous aspect of inquiry-based leadership is that we are making problematic our relationship to problem solving. (Maisterra, 2017)

Leading from an inquiry stance thus changes our conception of the day job, responding in ways more consistent with the complex contexts in which leaders operate today. It requires, for instance, the questioning of taken-for-granted routines, which may carry broader social justice and equity implications. Another author reflects:

> As leaders, we are all taking risks in our practice to attempt to navigate a system that is layered with dysfunction. We are all questioning our own practice and the practice of those around us, with the intention of instituting positive change for young people. (Speller, 2017)

Such an approach to leadership can, therefore, help to surface difficult social and cultural issues, unearthing richly complex dynamics affecting the school community. In this way, leaders more transparently engage with aspects of education's relationship with our society's ambitions for social equity, democratic vitality, and human flourishing. They uncover previously unstated problems and opportunities, including messy ties across the institutions, communities, and profession they inhabit. This enlarges and complicates their work, embedding uncertainty and challenge but also enlivening it, placing it more securely within larger, fundamental issues and making it a more explicit part of a local community's discourse. Framed in this way, inquiry "is not as much about solution as it is about learning" (Tennant, 2017).

Enhancing the roles of educational leaders, then, moves beyond merely increasing recognition of their professionalism; it also recovers just a bit of the more integral role the public's education is meant to serve in a democratic republic aspiring to greater equity and justice. While this may be off-putting to some, it counters the often demotivating, instrumentalist approaches prompting far too many talented leaders to exit the field today. Deepening the importance of these issues as central to leading thus raises considerations about who might be attracted to lead communities and schools and how to better prepare them to lead in this way.

Rethinking Approaches to Leader Recruitment and Development

An enhanced conception of educational leadership, in turn, calls for enhanced approaches to recruitment, preparation, and support, potentially drawing upon a much wider range of disciplinary resources and insights. It raises important questions for both leaders and those who educate and support them: What are the personal challenges involved should leading from an inquiry stance be embraced, and how do we as a field support increased comfort with ambiguity, uncertainty, and vulnerability? How do we support leaders' agency, their ability to collectively engage a diverse and even contentious community in inquiry? How might we better develop our ability to listen, prod, and listen again in ways difficult to sustain at times but in service of moving past "the polarization of ideologies . . . [and in]

recognition of the importance of fostering civic discourse and authentic dialogue" (Cruice, 2017)?

To follow an inquiry stance, leaders must be able to draw upon a wider range of disciplinary resources and perspectives; the complexity of their context will require it. How might, for example, the disciplines of history and literature enhance leaders' ability to understand nuanced narratives of their community, to weave the multiple voices of any local story? In what ways might economics inform the reading of educational incentives at play within and outside of the community? In what ways could the arts assist in a deeper noticing, in bringing an aesthetic understanding to cultural tensions? What might leaders learn from being in inquiring communities with anthropologists who, as a discipline, explicitly work across cultural, racial, and class boundaries? How might leadership preparation programs curate, broker, and coordinate such a multidisciplinary approach to the development and ongoing support of leaders?

The Importance of Practitioner Knowledge Generation

Beyond recruitment, preparation, and support, leading from an inquiry stance—if taken up in the field—would imply shifts in the institutional and political infrastructure of educational policy to which leaders must attend. As leaders engage their community in collaborative inquiry, striving to make sense collectively of what affects their children's education, some of what they uncover may challenge existing interests, existing structures, and even existing decisionmakers. In the words of one of the authors of this volume, "inquiry shifts power and when a leader creates the space for such scrutiny, belief systems can be challenged" (Cruice, personal communication, 2017). How does knowledge originating from such inquiry then relate to other forms of knowledge that may be generated from outside the local context, and/or from more "official" sources? In what ways would newly empowered local constituents, at community and site levels, either complement, enhance, or be seen to potentially threaten current policy and political actors? Given the need for varying types of sense-making, not limited to that which is generated through local inquiry-based leadership, how would the field sustain multiple modalities of investigation? Would a new "politics of knowledge" need to emerge, or emerge on its own, should this work expand (Lagemann, 1989)?

The Raising of Leader Voices

Finally, leading from an inquiry stance implies expanded allowances for professional voice—an enlargement of ways to raise practitioner expertise into the public discourse on education. Inquiries draw educational leaders more directly into wider social issues, where their daily engagement may provide key perspectives for the public. As local communities inquire into schooling practices, they are able to provide insights, for example, on how policies of immigration, social welfare, and health care play out in real communities. Leaders facilitating these inquiries can look to contribute what is learned locally in new ways. School leaders/practitioners, and those whom they engage in local inquiry, may be called upon increasingly to raise their voices in several directions—via social media networking, publishing, presenting, blogging, and leading professional development. In this way, the professional discourse may broaden and become less parochial, spilling beyond the narrow bounds of one's position or role. In response, organizations supporting leaders—from districts, to intermediate units, to departments of education, to universities—would need to find more ways to support and share this practitioner-generated work.

Clearly, we can only speculate regarding the implications of an expanded conception of educational leadership from an inquiry stance. Only our ongoing collective inquiry as a field will determine these implications, as a community is created that is committed to the integration of practitioner-generated sensemaking within "standard" leadership practice.

Within the inquiry stance framework, and in light of these wider potential implications, how might leaders—new and experienced—emerge from and lead from different spaces in an organization with a culture of inquiry?

CONSIDERATIONS FOR LEADERSHIP DEVELOPMENT AND PRACTICE

We hope that this book can potentially open up conversations about how leaders see, understand, make sense of, respond to, improve, and possibly disrupt the life of the school or organization as a leader. *Repositioning Educational Leadership* is thus intended to be read and discussed among educational leaders at varying levels of experience—in, for example, district meetings, professional development settings, graduate courses, masters and doctoral programs, and principal-to-principal collaboration. In reading and discussing the book, leaders and prospective leaders might take up such questions as: What prompts inquiry? How are these chapters invitations to the productive possibilities of this approach? How might educational leaders take an inquiry stance in a range of different contexts to identify and act on critical issues in their institutions, their communities, and beyond? Additional questions to consider when reading this book (and when thinking and writing about one's own inquiry-based leadership) are included in Appendix A, a revised Practitioner Inquiry Framework, adapted for *Repositioning Educational Leadership*.

The 11 chapters in this volume provide a range of examples written by leaders in a variety of positions and contexts. From the outset, we and the practitioner-scholars who authored these chapters have been careful about making claims that specific outcomes or benefits could be attributed to taking an inquiry stance per se. Instead, what surprised us as we assembled the book was the strong connection among the authors' narratives, their ability to establish trusting relationships with others, and their connection to the students in their schools or districts. Whether principals, teacher leaders, or central office administrators, the authors were clear about how their inquiries were driven by concern for students and by interactions with them. When viewed from this perspective—the benefits or outcomes of leading from an inquiry stance—the chapters reveal a consistent orientation to improving conditions for teaching and learning.

We acknowledge that the three sets of chapters included in this book do not begin to capture the range and complexity of the work that school leaders do; they are only a sample. What the chapters do provide are compelling examples of how leaders in particular situations sensed or confronted a problem or challenge, adopted an inquiry stance, and took on that problem/challenge. Nevertheless, the question remains: "How might readers of this book go about identifying and choosing problems and challenges that merit inquiry?"

Earlier, we made the point that taking an inquiry stance offers "the potential for site-based leaders to identify (often with their colleagues, students, and parents in the community) issues and problems that are *locally* significant, previously unrecognized, and rarely given the systematic, intentional study that an inquiry-based approach to leadership affords." Inquiry can be prompted by problems posed that are specific to the particular context, and though previously unrecognized, may prompt further investigation. Thus, readers are also encouraged to question taken-for-granted policies, practices, and conventions.

Inquiry may emerge from the asking of more generic questions, posed by groups of school leaders across institutions in dialogue with others in the organization and community and in inquiry groups that create space to share data, analyses, and interpretations. To assist in that effort and prompt readers to conduct their own inquiries, we offer a few additional examples intended to stimulate thinking about potential inquiries that could be undertaken in one's own setting:

- What is "special" about special education at my school? (Is the pedagogy in special education classrooms demonstrably different?)
- What does it mean that our parent meetings are so poorly attended?
- How does our teacher evaluation system inform or shape teaching and learning and to what end?
- How do we make sense of teacher turnover in our school?

There are, of course, myriad questions that are worthy of inquiry and have the potential to improve practice and student outcomes in one's community and schools.

A significant part of responding to questions like these is figuring out how to go about inquiring into them, and this may look different for each individual, school, organization, or community. Additionally, accepting what emerges from an inquiry may initially be ambiguous or disquieting. On this challenge, Tennant (2017) reflects that "the understanding of this insider's . . . perspective gives a permission [he] did not previously allow [himself] in terms of the messiness of the work." Through inquiry, one leverages uncertainty toward generative ends.

AN INVITATION

Taking an inquiring stance can inspire "leaderly" acts: posing problems of practice (broadly construed) for which both the problem and the solution are not known; believing in and generating knowledge of the local and emanating from the questions and problems posed; and joining with others in the organization to explore and gather data to create a more comprehensive picture of what might be happening at various levels. Those who worked on this volume hope that we as a field can work together to further understand the practices of the locally attentive, empirically driven approach that is leadership from an inquiry stance, in all its upsides and challenges.

As our effort to date indicates, this carries significant implications for how we prepare leaders, how we support leaders, and the policy context in which we operate. This cannot be solely a single publication, nor solely a publication venture. Toward the promotion of a wider conversation, we invite you to help advance what we know and are able to do as a profession in developing this critical "third space" for the leaders of our shared educational work.

REFERENCES

Cochran-Smith, M., & Lytle, S. L. (1999). Relationships of knowledge and practice: Teacher learning in communities. In A. Iran-Nejad & P. David Pearson (Eds.), *Review of research in education, volume 24* (pp. 249–306). Washington, DC: American Educational Research Association.

Cochran-Smith, M., & Lytle, S. L. (2009). *Inquiry as stance: Practitioner research for the next generation*. New York, NY: Teachers College Press.

Cruice, P. A. (2017). Reflections presented at the second Leading from an Inquiry Stance Writing Retreat, June 2017, Philadelphia, PA.

Lagemann, E. C. (1989). *The politics of knowledge: The Carnegie Corporation, philanthropy, and public policy* (1st ed.). Middletown, CT: Wesleyan University Press.

Maisterra, A. (2017). Reflections presented at the second Leading from an Inquiry Stance Writing Retreat, June 2017, Philadelphia, PA.

Speller, M. T. (2017). Reflections presented at the second Leading from an Inquiry Stance Writing Retreat, June 2017, Philadelphia, PA.

Tennant, N. (2017). Reflections presented at the second Leading from an Inquiry Stance Writing Retreat, June 2017, Philadelphia, PA.

APPENDIX A

Reading, Writing, and Talking About Leading from an Inquiry Stance

As evidenced by the accounts of leadership included in this book, the work of inquiry in/on practice is intellectual, social, and political, occurring within webs of historical and cultural significance. That is, it involves making problematic the current conventions or arrangements of practice; the ways knowledge is constructed, evaluated, and used in various settings; and the roles leaders play in imagining and bringing about positive change in their own work contexts (Cochran-Smith & Lytle, 2009). The framework that follows offers leaders and prospective leaders questions to consider as readers and/or writers of practitioner accounts focused on inquiry-based leadership in schools and districts. It also introduces dimensions of planning and enacting practitioner inquiry that may be useful for leaders confronted with a challenge or problem that invites consideration from a stance of inquiry.

The left-hand column is specifically about reading—that is, questions for readers to ask about chapters (like those in this book) or articles written about leadership as a form of inquiry in publications such as educational journals, blogs, or monographs. As we hope the 11 practitioner-authored chapters in this book make clear, although there are generic questions to consider, every situation or context is unique and needs to be approached with that assumption as a starting point.

The right-hand column focuses on writing—that is, questions for writers to ask themselves that may be important to think about in crafting their own leadership narratives of experiences leading from an inquiry stance. As editors of this volume, we are hoping that many differently situated leaders will be encouraged to compose their own narrative analyses of critical experiences in a range of educational contexts and from varied perspectives and to disseminate them both locally and more widely.

Overall, the table offers a framework supporting the analysis and writing of texts that address important problems in the field from leaders' perspectives and enhance practitioners' participation in knowledge generation for the field. It is intended to be used by individual leaders, study groups, members of school or system leadership teams, participants in certification programs and courses in master's or doctoral programs for educational leaders, public sector or community organization–based educators, as well as professional development programs for leaders.

PRACTITIONER INQUIRY: A FRAMEWORK
Leading from an Inquiry Stance

Reading Practitioner Inquiry on Leadership	Writing about Leadership as Inquiry
LEGACY	
Where do these leadership acts come from? What educational problems is this work connected to, and how/why does this matter?	Where do I come from? What are my social, cultural, political, and educational frameworks? What traditions, disciplines, or educational histories do I come from, and how/why does this matter? What is my experience with writing about my leadership?
LOCATION/POSITIONALITY	
Who is doing this work and where is the work being done? What are the relationships among the participants? What perspectives do they bring? How does the leader position himself/herself in this inquiry?	Who am I to be doing this work? What is my location in the work? Is my leadership stance with/for/about others? To what extent and in what ways is my leadership work intended to be collaborative/participatory? How is my positionality defined by others? Who are the "others"?
WAYS OF KNOWING	
How does this insider story of leading from an inquiry stance inform what I as reader think about my own leadership? How is this "local knowledge" and how is it also "global"?	What assumptions am I making about knowers and the nature of knowledge? What do I understand as the relationships of knowledge and practice? How do I position myself/others as generators of knowledge?

Reading Practitioner Inquiry on Leadership	**Writing about Leadership as Inquiry**
ORIENTATION	
What is this story of leadership about? Who is it for? Why? What role do questions play in this process? Whose questions are salient?	What aspect(s) of my leadership am I writing about? What is my purpose(s) in doing this writing? How did I frame questions to guide my inquiry? How did these questions evolve throughout the process of the inquiry?
METHODS	
What kind of story is this? What kinds of "data" is the chapter author using? How are these data collected, analyzed, and interpreted? By whom?	What genre of article/chapter am I writing? What kinds of information or data of practice do I need to tell the story—and how will I collect, organize, analyze, and interpret them? What ethical issues will/may arise during this writing?
COMMUNITY	
What is the social organization of the leadership stance described here? What are the communities to which the writer/leader belongs? Why (and how) do these matter?	What is the social organization of the work? What are the communities to which I belong? Why do these matter? How is the community in which I am the leader responding to my leading from an inquiry stance?
NEIGHBORHOOD	
Who is the audience for this chapter? Why does this matter?	Who am I/are we talking to in my chapter? Why does this matter?

Adapted from a handout prepared by Susan L. Lytle for Education 669, Practitioner Inquiry, at the University of Pennsylvania Graduate School of Education.

REFERENCE

Cochran-Smith, M., & Lytle, S. L. (2009). *Inquiry as stance: Practitioner research for the next generation*. New York, NY: Teachers College Press.

The Mid-Career Doctoral Program in Educational Leadership

While this volume is not about a specific program, it has its genesis in the editors' shared experience at a research university as faculty and staff of a doctoral program for veteran educational leaders, the **Mid-Career Doctoral Program in Educational Leadership (Mid-Career Program)** at the University of Pennsylvania Graduate School of Education (Penn GSE). Begun in 2002, the Mid-Career Program serves a select national network of experienced educational leaders from public and private sectors, pre-K–12, through an intensive, cohort-based, 3-year program characterized by

- Practitioner- and inquiry-based focus;
- Lifetime access to program supports;
- On-demand access to writing, research, and social media coaches; and
- Executive format classes meeting one weekend a month.

The program objectives are twofold:

1. *Enhance and deepen the leadership repertoire of our students and alumni.* Simply, we aim to develop our colleagues as stronger leaders in their current organizations, and in their subsequent organizations.
2. *Support our network in their leadership to the wider field.* Part of leadership sits squarely in one's immediate institution and community. Yet as a community we see that as insufficient, and continue to develop productive, generative means by which our alumni can amplify their impact on the wider educational landscape. We provide a makerspace for our students and alumni: a place to create, develop, and refine initiatives that benefit our practice and those we serve, as well as the wider field of pre-K–12 education.

As noted in the introduction, the network includes independent school heads, department heads, teacher-leaders, charter school founders, superintendents, national association leaders, non-profit leaders, entrepreneurs, state education department administrators, and other leaders in the pre-K–12 world. Each school leader brings on average 18 years of experience to the table; each cohort of 25 leaders draws from over a dozen states and brings roughly 450 years of experience. The community of students, alumni, program faculty, and associates represent an intentionally sought, presumption-challenging diversity of race, gender, age, discipline, position, locale, ideology, geography, and career path. The cohort format grounds the work in mutual respect across the differences of background, perspective, and context, while modeling the engagement of peers in problem-posing and dialogic inquiry.

In this 3-year program, participants learn about and engage in professional, site-based inquiries throughout their coursework, identifying and investigating significant problems that emerge from their everyday practice with the expressed goal of contributing to educational improvement, both within and beyond their own settings. The program has learned that

> participation in these communities offers a context for raising questions and deepening participants' understanding of critical issues in leadership broadly and in their own leadership context specifically. This is important because it affords students, who are seasoned professionals, an ongoing site for examining their own issues and questions of practice and also puts them in continuous dialogue with a diverse group of educational leaders with similar and different issues and concerns. (Ravitch & Lytle, 2016, p. 148)

The cohort nature of the program is thus a critical aspect; classes are grounded in respect for individuals' prior and current experiences and the knowledge they bring to the conversation from across their work and perspectives.

Penn GSE's Mid-Career Program embraces collaboration and reflective practice explicitly. The distinctive focus on inquiry-based educational leadership offers a significant departure from most other doctoral programs in the same field, and our curriculum addresses the ongoing transformation of public and private educational organizations by focusing specifically on the challenges faced by school and other educational leaders through four core lenses—instructional, organizational, public, and evidence based. This approach fosters a deep understanding of organizations, instruction, and learning, and of their implications for school.

Relatedly, the dissertation research conducted in the Mid-Career Program may be distinct from that done in other programs and research paradigms in the following ways:

1. Research questions are complex, highly contextualized, and deeply relevant to the researcher's background, role, and responsibilities within their settings.
2. Research problems are rigorously contextualized in the wider literature on leadership.
3. Significantly more diverse and in-depth data are collected (not just a problem described and solutions tested), in part because the researcher, as an insider within the setting, has unusual access.

4. Analysis of data reflects the conceptual frameworks of the researcher, his or her insider understandings, as well as the related academic literature.
5. There is considerably more benefit to the doctoral cohort from the dissertations of individual students because there is significant effort to convene inquiry communities and to make the process critical, collaborative, and dialogic. (Cochran-Smith & Lytle, 1999, 2009, as cited in Ravitch & Lytle, 2016, p. 148)

In sum, the collective mission is to educate practitioner-scholars who make significant contributions both to practice and to the scholarship of practice—that is, to the *scholarship of leading.* In a world usually sorted into knowledge-generators versus implementers, this program represents a constructive disruption of some understandings of the relationships of knowledge and practice, in and out of the university. The scholarship of leading foregrounds school and other educational leaders as knowledge generators and posits the Mid-Career Program as a practitioner-scholar community of current participants and graduates wherein students and faculty identify critical problems of practice that merit systematic and intentional inquiry, carry out those studies, and seek appropriate venues for dissemination (see Johanek & Lytle, 2010).

Just as this inquiry stance requires an embrace of uncertainty for our students, it requires the same from the program faculty and staff—an inquiry stance to our work, an engagement with our students and alumni about our shared ambitions and challenges. Penn GSE faculty play an integral and hands-on role in the leadership and development of the Mid-Career Doctoral Program. Led by a faculty steering committee, the program leadership regularly revises program design and curricular elements, coaching/staffing supports, technical infrastructure, and extensions into the field. The program continues to learn about what an inquiry stance involves for leaders, especially given the vast array of roles, contexts and institutions.

This constant learning has generated visible artifacts—one is this book, an important resource for surfacing the knowledge-generation of practitioners, and thus advancing their wider collective leadership for the field. Additionally, we continue to develop a portfolio of network initiatives, driven by member interests, through which we seek to serve the broader profession. We intend to foster increased attention to intergenerational (including alumni) cohort involvement in inquiry and to multiple avenues for dissemination of knowledge related to leadership in a range of contexts and media. Tapping into decades of practitioner experience, we build out concrete tools, research, and opportunities for networking and exchange to engage all our pre-K–12 colleagues.

The Mid-Career Program's varied network initiatives extend beyond the academic components of the doctoral experience. Each supports growth and learning across the leadership lifespan. These initiatives provide Mid-Career students, alumni, and faculty as well as invited guests with opportunities to share and amplify their impact in the wider pre-K–12 field and related sectors. We are committed to deepening the leadership repertoire of this community, and to investing in the development of others.

We support a renewed peer infrastructure of change. The Mid-Career Program is deeply committed to serving as a makerspace for members of our network and the wider pre-K–12 field. We are building the infrastructure of a multifaceted and geographically diverse network of practitioner scholars by supporting strategic, cross-sector collaborations. Committed to equity and diversity, our member-led network initiatives build directly from the interests, experience, and expertise of students, alumni, and friends. This growing set of efforts attempts to capture and scale out the otherwise hidden, tacit knowledge and wisdom of veteran leaders across a diverse range of educational contexts.

We focus on strengthening the leadership of individuals as well as their development of others in three distinct ways: by capturing insights on professional experience, learning through peer networks, and growing a global profession.

We invite you to visit the program website, *midcareer.gse.upenn.edu*, for further information on the program and its network initiatives.

REFERENCES

Johanek, M., & Lytle, J. (2010). Reinventing leaders for a new era in education management. *District Management Journal, 5*, 22–28.

Ravitch, S. M., & Lytle, S. L. (2016). Becoming practitioner-scholars: The role of practice-based inquiry dissertations in the development of educational leaders. In V. Storey & K. Hesbol (Eds.), *Contemporary approaches to dissertation development and research methods* (pp. 146–161). Hershey, PA: IGI Global.

About the Editors

James H. Lytle, EdD

Dr. J. H. "Torch" Lytle is adjunct practice professor of educational leadership at the University of Pennsylvania Graduate School of Education (Penn GSE). He has had extensive experience as an urban school administrator and has taught at Penn GSE for many years. His research interests relate to increasing the efficacy of urban public schools, managing leadership transitions, and leading school change efforts. J. H. Lytle received his doctorate in education from Stanford, a master's degree in English from the State University of New York at Buffalo, and his bachelor's degree from Cornell University.

Susan L. Lytle, PhD

Dr. S. L. Lytle is professor emerita of education at the University of Pennsylvania Graduate School of Education. She has been director of Penn GSE's master's and doctoral programs in Reading/Writing/Literacy, founding director of the Philadelphia Writing Project, and has published widely on topics related to literacy education, teacher learning and leadership, school-university partnerships, and practitioner inquiry. S. L. Lytle received her PhD in reading/writing/literacy from the University of Pennsylvania, an MA in English/education from Stanford University, and a BA in English from Cornell University.

Michael C. Johanek, EdD

Dr. Johanek, senior fellow at the University of Pennsylvania Graduate School of Education, directs Penn GSE's Mid-Career Doctoral Program in Educational Leadership (Mid-Career Program). He has extensive experience in the K–12, corporate, and not-for-profit education sectors, and his numerous publications focus on issues of civic education, educational leadership, school-community ties, and the history of U.S. education. Dr. Johanek earned an EdD in history and education and an MA in teaching of social studies from Teachers College, Columbia University, and has a BA in economics from Georgetown University.

Kathy J. Rho, EdD

Dr. Rho currently serves as the assistant director of the Mid-Career Program at the University of Pennsylvania Graduate School of Education. Before coming to Penn, she was an education program manager for a state-wide workforce development and education agency. Her current research focuses on the influence of social identities on school leadership thinking and practice. Dr. Rho received her doctorate in educational leadership from the University of Pennsylvania, a master's in education from Harvard University, and her bachelor's degree from Smith College.

Index